iBaby

a memoir

Idell Koury

HIGH BRIDGE BOOKS

iBaby
by Idell Koury

Copyright © 2023 by Idell Koury

All rights reserved.

Printed in the United States of America
ISBN: 978-1-954943-85-8

All scripture marked NIV is taken from THE HOLY BIBLE, NEW INTERNATIONAL VERSION®, NIV® Copyright © 1973, 1978, 1984, 2011 by Biblica, Inc.® Used by permission. All rights reserved worldwide.

Scripture quotations marked ESV are from The ESV® Bible (The Holy Bible, English Standard Version®), © 2001 by Crossway, a publishing ministry of Good News Publishers. Used by permission. All rights reserved.

High Bridge Books titles may be purchased in bulk for educational, business, fundraising, or sales promotional use. For information, please contact High Bridge Books via www.highbridgebooks.com/contact.

Published in Houston, Texas by High Bridge Books.

Dedication

This book is dedicated to my mom who met her Savior in June 2023. God welcomed her home. He allowed me to be with her as He welcomed her into Heaven. Momma overcame many obstacles, received Christ, transformed her mind, and pointed me to God. You are wearing a crown now, Mom.

OBITUARIES
Amalia Revell

Amalia Baca Revell

August 6, 1922 – June 26, 2023
It is with heavy hearts that we announce the passing of Amalia Baca Revell – affectionately known to her friends and family as "Molly." Amalia was born in 1922 to Delfinia Chavez and Max Baca, Sr. in Albuquerque. A life-long resident of New Mexico, Amalia was a friend to all and loved by all of those who had the fortune to know her. Kind beyond words, she touched the lives of so many in her 100+ years on earth. She was a beautiful woman, a devout Catholic and had a zest for life without preten-tiousness. Amalia was preceded in death by her children Patricia and Ronnie. She is survived by her daughters Louise, Linda, Idell, Daryl, Sylvia, 17 grandchildren and many great grand-children. Pall bearers who were honored to carry her to her final resting place at Mount Calvary Cemetery were Richard Enriquez, Tony Koury, Ken Mashke, Manuel Griego, Josh Mashke and Avelino Apodaca. May you rest in peace. Mom. To view Amalia's full obituary and view/con-tribute photos and trib-utes please visit www.salazarfunerals.com.

Contents

Acknowledgments   vii

Introduction   1

1. Abiquiu and Apples   3

2. San Felipe School in Old Town, Albuquerque   9

3. The Little Red Wagon   13

4. Foster Home   17

5. Ronnie and Vietnam   21

6. Life in the Projects   25

7. Where Have All the Good Men Gone?   29

8. Joseph Herring   35

9. NMSU, UNM, and EDPA   39

10. Daddy and D.C.   45

11. Capitol Hill   51

12. Baseball on the Hill   59

13. The Blind Date   61

14. TAG   65

15. "Rocky Roads"   73

16. Marriage   79

17. California   83

18. Focal Point   87

19. Twins   91

20. The Challenge   95

21. God's Provision   101

22. Spirits and Maryland   103

23. Filling Our Home   107

24. Centennial and Truth   111

25. Activism   115

26. Signs and Wonders   117

27. Daddy Dies   121

28. South Carolina   125

29. Hurricane Hugo and River Walk   127

30. The Campaign   131

31. Trailer Park   135

32. One Friday Night   137

33. James Madison Memorial Fellowship   141

34. SCS Again   147

35. 23rd Psalm   149

Epilogue   153

Citations   155

Acknowledgments

I owe much to my two older sisters, Louise and Linda, and my husband, Tony. Linda saved my physical life when she took me to the hospital in a little red wagon as I was knocking on death's door. Tony introduced me to a new way of life.

Louise, my oldest sister, saved my emotional life when I rejected our poor surroundings in low-income housing twice. Then a third time when I was attending the University of New Mexico. Louise has always been my confidante. I love you, Louise, and thank you. I will always depend on my older sisters for their calm and for their clarity.

I would also like to thank my mom and dad. My dad, Archie Lloyd Sandidge Revell, was my best friend when he was with us. I know parents are not to show favoritism, but I felt special to my dad. I felt as though he loved me very much as his firstborn. My mom, Amalia Baca Chavez Revell, asked me to wait to publish this book because it contains many painful memories. I have honored her wish. This book was published after Mom met her Savior face to face. She was an inspiration as she overcame many obstacles.

I want to thank my mom for sharing her faith with me. She sent her three little girls to Catholic school even though her husband, my dad, was agnostic. Daddy did not believe in Christ nor have mom's faith, but he still sent us to Catholic school. I learned so much from the nuns and the lay teachers at San Felipe, St. Thomas, and Holy Cross Catholic Schools. I learned so much about faith, repentance, daily discipline, true love, patience, and forgiveness from my mom. Thank you, Mom. I know you cannot read this now, but you laid the foundation of my faith. I love you. God does, too.

Thank you, Tony, for being obedient and giving me the opportunity to acknowledge and confess my past, receive salvation, and renew my mind. You have repeatedly encouraged me to author this book. You bought me a new computer and equipped me with other resources. You give to me what I need. I love you. I am grateful.

Introduction

How did a poor little Hispanic girl, born 30 miles from the Mexican border town of El Paso and Ciudad Juarez, converse with a U.S. president as an official representative, get escorted up the wedding aisle by a U.S. Senator from New Mexico, and run a friend's unlikely but successful campaign for Greenville County School Board in South Carolina?

This book is entitled *iBaby*. It was a name Daddy always called me. I was his firstborn biological child, and he doted on me. He spent time with me when I was young. I feel sorry for those who have never experienced a father's love. When he left, it was very hard to reconcile this love and dedication to his absence for so many years. I know that I will see Daddy again because of his submission to Christ after he spent a lifetime of resistance.

God placed certain people in my path to direct my steps. Linda, my older sister, saved my physical life. She was only 12, and I was nine. Louise saved my emotional life many times. They have always been clear thinkers and unselfish. Linda was my example in parenting as I spent many days at her house when she had four little children. Louise was my professional encourager. Louise would just listen and encourage me. As my older sisters, Linda and Louise played a significant role in my upbringing. As half-sisters who had every reason to distance themselves from my biological dad and me, they did not. They were, and still are, gracious and kind human beings.

My dad, Archie Lloyd Revell, was unique. He was also an agnostic and a scoundrel. As Tony put it after he met him for the first time, Daddy acted like a modern-day Archie Bunker. My dad left my mom, was probably a bigamist, and was opinionated. He also loved his I baby, me. I felt it, and I knew it to be truth as I spent years with him. God had to take him away for His purposes. I would have grown up to be just like Daddy.

1

Abiquiu and Apples

When I was young, we lived in Abiquiu, in northern New Mexico. Abiquiu is northwest of the capital city of Santa Fe. It is a picturesque town full of adventure-seekers and artists in Rio Arriba County. Abiquiu was the home of the famed artist, Georgia O'Keeffe, who lived there from 1949 to 1986. We lived there during that time but did not know O'Keeffe. *Only In Your State* website wrote about Abiquiu:

> New Mexican landscapes are associated with dramatic rock formations and vibrant colors. Although the bar for breath-taking scenery is set high, there is one place where the colors are a little deeper and the natural beauty halts even the most jaded travelers in their tracks. Offering a natural amphithea-ter, a lake, a lavender farm, and a unique history, the town of Abiquiu…[1]

Abiquiu was also near the lowriders' haven of Española. Lowriders are what we called mostly Hispanics who cruised their cars with low-to-the-ground frames. Their mirrors, wheels, and sometimes windows were decorated with lights, dingo balls, and other things. There were and still are many Hispanics in northern New Mexico. There are still lowriders, too. Our family spent many years in northern New Mexico. My sisters still live there. And there are still many lowriders.

Our family's move to Abiquiu in northern New Mexico was for a new job of harvesting and selling apples from a 100-tree apple orchard. My daddy was considered a "Jack of all trades" and wanted to harvest and sell apples. When my two sisters and I were not fishing in the Chama River, we spent time climbing the apple trees. During the fall harvest that year, we joined my dad and sat in the back of his truck to sell apples to people as they drove by. We sold them by bag, bushel, or basket. We sold varieties of northern New Mexico apples.

One time my older sister, Linda, fled as she ran fast around our house in Abiquiu with terror on her face. I sat and watched in amazement and curiosity as I witnessed my slightly overweight dad running after Linda. His face was red. I thought the redness was from his fast and belabored running. That contributed to the strained look, I supposed. I also noticed, however, a large bump between Daddy's eyes. I found out later that my sister had wrapped a rock in a mudball and, accidentally, hit Daddy as she aimed at my other sister. I do not remember much after my sister's crying plea for help when my dad finally caught her. My mom, in typical fashion, pleaded for leniency for her when Linda ran into the house to seek protection from Momma.

My mom made friends easily. She spent time with a neighbor in Abiquiu named Lodgie. She came to our home to visit often. This was a time before new sexual orientations were a thing in culture. Now, she might be considered a man. She dressed like one and acted like one. She seemed to be happily married to a man, however, and considered herself a woman. She was gruff in some ways but was a good conversationalist. Lodgie seemed genuinely impressed when I told her about the chicks we were raising in the spare bedroom. She seemed impressed that we would feed them cornbread daily to help them receive nourishment and grow into chickens.

Lodgie was also amused when I told her I once killed a Gila monster near our outhouse. (We did not have an indoor bathroom in Abiquiu. We would bundle up and walk out to get to our outhouse.) I told Lodgie that I picked up a large stone and killed the Gila monster. I later found out it was a poisonous lizard. Lodgie and my mom were friends, and I felt that I could tell Lodgie anything. She seemed intrigued when I recounted one fishing experience I had with my family.

I had been fishing in the Chama River with my parents and sisters. My desire was to run to where my mom and sisters went as they had walked upstream while I stayed with Daddy to catch fish. I remember trying to run on the rocky riverbank when a large rock moved. Under the rock slithered a nest of little rattlesnakes. My dad warned us that baby rattlesnakes were just as venomous as grown rattlesnakes. I stood there frozen. I watched the little creatures crawl across my shoes as I stiffly listened to my dad scream, "I baby, I baby!" It turned out that my frozen stance was what saved me from multiple snake bites. The baby snakes perceived that I was not a threat and slithered down to the riverbank. I can still see the little snakes crawling across my shoes. I still get queasy when I see a snake. My first instinct today is to kill a snake (whether it's harmless or not) so it will not hurt anyone.

Although we lived there only a brief time, I have vivid memories of going up the hill to old town Abiquiu and attending the Saint Tomas Catholic School (which no longer exists). Second and third grades were combined in one classroom as it was a small school. I thought it was cool to have another grade in my class. It reminded me of the one-room schoolhouses I had read about so much in books.

Santa Tomás de Apostle Parish Catholic Church once governed the school. There is a rich history of the Parish. As Annelida Dunning wrote in 2018,

> …Most of Abiquiu's history revolves around the church. One thing that comes across loud and clear when discussing the history of Santa Tomás de Apostle in Abiquiu is that it was the tenacity, perseverance and fortitude of the people that have kept it thriving … There is a devotion and pride of place that flows through the veins of the people of Santa Tomás de Apostle de Abiquiu Catholic Church.[2]

Lodgie's tenacity, perseverance, and pride of her home was an example of what Annelida wrote. Lodgie made an impression on me. She was a cowgirl but was kind and a good listener. I remember telling Lodgie about duck hunting early in the morning with my dad. I have great memories of hunting with Daddy as we waded through the reeds. We waited quietly and whispered about life until we saw a flock of ducks fly in front of us. I was too young to shoot but remember seeing my dad shoot at the flock. I do not remember if he shot a duck, but I have warm memories of hunting with him. It was just me and my daddy in the early morning. It remains a special memory.

My childhood memories include trout fishing many times with my dad. We would catch the fish, and my dad would cook the fish on a campfire. Our experiences probably prevented my older sister, Linda, from complaining when she spent her honeymoon in a tent in Questa, NM. She was accustomed to camping even though we slept in my dad's old Cadillac, not a tent.

I clearly remember my mom calling us to the front of my dad's car to take a picture. I was not happy as I had just caught a trout in the mountain stream. I had been fishing all morning. It took patience as we did not own fancy fishing rods or tackle boxes. We usually used a long stick, a fishing line, and a hook. I was disappointed because I had to let the fish go but obeyed my dad when he called, "I baby." My mom took the photo, but I was not happy as can be seen. Nevertheless, I have good memories of Abiquiu.

My dad, Archie Lloyd Revell, with his three daughters fishing in Abiquiu. I was not happy about leaving my freshly caught trout.

We used to take hikes up the backside of Battleship Rock, a rock formation that looked like a battleship near Abiquiu in the Jemez Mountains. My mom was not happy about those hikes. I remember one hike we took with our friends Stella and her son, Jimmy Bentley. Mom was fearful. No … she was hysterical when we leaned over the top and waved down to her with our friends. I must admit that seeing my mom's hysterical reaction gave me pause to continue looking down as I waved down to her. We did not stay at the top exceedingly long but hurried down the back of the rock.

We loved hiking, and my dad often took us to camp or hike when we were young.

My parents loved each other. My mom wrote many notes and letters to me. She chronicled their relationship and assured me that she really loved Daddy. In one of the hundreds of notes, she told of their brief courtship and her happiness.

2

San Felipe School in Old Town, Albuquerque

My family moved often, but Mom always enrolled us in Catholic school. Once when we moved back to Albuquerque, Daddy said he was going on a "trip." My dad went on "trips" frequently. I did not know where he went but was always happy when he returned.

On his previous "trip" when we lived in Albuquerque, I came home from San Felipe Elementary School. Mom enrolled us at the Catholic Church school that is still operating in Old Town, and we moved across from the school so we could walk. The Catholic school is still called San Felipe Catholic School and is under the auspices of San Felipe de Neri Catholic Church where I received my first Holy Communion and was confirmed in the Catholic Church.

I walked home from San Felipe Elementary School and saw a man on a motorcycle in front of me. I quickly walked past him as I knew I should not talk to strangers. As I quickly walked past, I heard a familiar voice call, "I baby, I baby." There was only one person who called me "I baby." I knew it was my

My confirmation picture at San Felipe Catholic Church

daddy, and I ran to him. I almost knocked him over on his motorcycle but was so happy he had come back that I did not care if we fell over.

We walked into the apartment together where my mom was cooking white navy beans. I remember Daddy being upset that we were eating beans for dinner but did not think much about it as I was just happy he came home.

I do not remember much about Daddy's interaction with Momma. I just remember Momma being happy that Daddy was home and would again provide for us.

Daddy bought a Cadillac while we lived near San Felipe. Linda decided to "drive" it down the hill. Daddy had a red face as he ran behind the car trying to stop us. I do recall thinking to myself that there was no reason

Tony and me in front of San Felipe Church in Old Town, Albuquerque

for Daddy to be so upset. We were just taking a joyride down the hill, and Linda was a good driver. She had common sense. Why didn't Daddy trust her driving his car at her young age? She was almost nine, I thought.

After all, Linda had once saved my life on another occasion when Daddy's Cadillac went around a corner and the door flew open next to me as I sat in the seat without a seatbelt. Linda just nonchalantly reached over and grabbed my waistband as I slid out the car door. I did not know why Daddy was so red in the face, again.

Yet another time, Linda was "pretending" to drive in our parking spot behind our house on Edith Street in Albuquerque. We were sitting in the front seat, and Linda "accidentally" put Daddy's Cadillac in reverse and rolled backward into the taxicab stand's trash cans across the alley. Again, daddy was red-faced as he screamed at his girls to stop. Linda knew what to do in a crisis. She always did. She had common sense.

Once when we lived near San Felipe Elementary School, I walked home to meet Richard Boone in the late 1950s. He starred in the hit western series *Have Gun Will Travel*. Mr. Boone must have been in Old Town shooting a cowboy film. Anyway, he met us at a hotel near Old Town and gave us finger rings because he thought we were cute or he had just made friends with Daddy. I do not know. I just remember thinking that he was a nice Hollywood actor.

We lived next to the Albuquerque library on Edith Street for a few years. My dad always took us to get our library card when we moved. He loved books and was an avid reader. Reading was important to Daddy. He had many books on his shelf and could converse about most subjects. I remember him taking me on some of his "trips" as he hauled bricks and other items. The nuns were not happy about my absences from school. When they complained to Daddy, he replied, "My I baby is getting a better education with me than she will ever get with you!"

Well, I thought, that settles that, and walked off holding hands with Daddy. He had answered his critics.

My daddy did a lot for us. I remember him setting out three stacks of coins when we lived on Edith Street and needed a ride to school. There were tokens for us to use to ride the bus to and from San Felipe Catholic School. The other coins were for our lunch. I remember him buying life-size dolls one Christmas. They were big and my size. I remember how happy I felt when I saw the dolls. My mom never let us forget that special Christmas.

One time, we sat at a bar, and I watched Daddy converse with other patrons. He never drank alcohol but smoked cigarettes like a train. Daddy smoked a pack of unfiltered cigarettes daily. He smoked the brands Lucky Strike and Marlboro. We knew nothing about secondhand smoke dangers. I was exposed to toxic secondhand smoke as I was always with him when we were both at home.

I recall Daddy defending my right to join in the political discussion about the upcoming election. Daddy knew about all the heroic actions of Dwight D. Eisenhower in World War II. He was not as sure about the election of John F. Kennedy (JFK). He knew JFK's heroism in the PT-109 saga but had reservations about JFK's dad, Joseph Sr., who was a philanderer, a Nazi, and a Senator McCarthy sympathizer, and Mr. Joseph Kennedy had his own daughter lobotomized because of political ambition. My daddy could not trust a candidate who exchanged human life for ambition. JFK was a staunch anti-Communist, our new enemy, but daddy was leery of JFK as U.S. president. He knew that JFK's younger brother, Robert F. Kennedy (whom JFK later appointed as U.S. attorney general), would go after organized crime but was leery of JFK's pedigree. His dad, Joseph Sr., had raised his sons to be philanderers like he was. My daddy was agnostic but had a moral streak that came from somewhere. He did not trust cheater politicians. He believed cheater politicians could not be trusted with a vote.

I enjoyed the conversations, learned much, and enjoyed listening to Daddy's discussions. That is why I have always enjoyed political discussion. I was allowed to join the political discussion at an early age. That is why I loved working for a U.S. Congressman and a U.S. Senator, chaired a successful campaign, and was encouraged to run for the South Carolina State House by another legislator. I love political discussions and was unafraid to discuss any topic. I learned at a young age, and my ideas were accepted.

I have some painful memories of when we lived in Albuquerque, too. Daddy's hatred of infidelity explains his reaction at finding another man in our house with my mom. Bolo was his name, and he came to visit after my dad went to work at night. Daddy found Bolo with my mom when he came home from work. He worked as a Yellow Cab driver in Albuquerque at night when we lived on Edith Street. I remember Daddy's anger and physical hostility when he came home from work. I watched and hid as Daddy took out his anger on Momma. He grabbed her by the hair and dragged her into the alley behind our house. He was angry at the infidelity. He was angry that it was done in front of his three girls. I was angry and afraid as I hid behind the steps in front of our house on Edith Street. I also knew Bolo was wrong to be with my mom when my dad worked.

I remember kicking him in the shins and yelling at him, "You are not my daddy! You must leave!"

I was young but inherited a sense of right and wrong from my agnostic dad. Bolo visiting my mom was clearly very wrong. Infidelity was wrong. Drunkenness was wrong. I inherited the moral code of my dad. He left us after the incident with Bolo.

3

The Little Red Wagon

Daddy came back, and we moved into a mobile home near Las Cruces, New Mexico. Daddy told us he was going on a "trip" and would be back for his girls. He left that night, and Momma moved to another apartment.

Momma then enrolled us at Holy Cross Elementary School in Las Cruces. We went to school daily and came home to find Momma with another man named Raymundo. I was confused and angry at the sight of Raymundo at our home with my mom. We were on public welfare because we had no income after Daddy left. Our welfare check was being spent on alcohol to appease my mom's new friend. I knew it was wrong to spend our limited funds on alcohol. I knew it was wrong to be disloyal to my daddy and he would be angry when he returned. Daddy hated booze and infidelity, and I did, too. We played outside a lot, and we went to school. I was confused but loved both our parents. I just could not understand it all.

Once when I was hungry as I walked home after school, I ate something that was in the rotting trash. I was very hungry, and no adult was around to teach and talk to me. I thought it was okay because it looked okay. I do not know how long the thrown-away food was in the trash. I got extremely sick after my "snack." I was very nauseated, threw up often, and had diarrhea.

I was sick for many days. The nuns at Holy Cross School in Las Cruces sent notes home about my absence. My mom was concerned and gave me Epsom Salts to try to stop the vomiting and diarrhea. I remember sitting on the outside front step of our house thinking I was going to die one evening. My mom was with Raymundo (or Badu as we called him). He came into my mom's life during Dad's "absence." I do remember missing Daddy terribly during this time. I knew he would take care of his I baby.

My sister, Linda, decided to act. She secured a red wagon and made it comfortable for me with blankets and a pillow. She was going to take her extremely sick little sister to the hospital. I do not remember much of the ride. I do remember the sun was shining as we rode, however. I remember a nice lady's voice.

There was also an angry man's voice. The emergency room doctor met us in the lobby. A kind lady near Memorial Hospital saw my sister, Linda, pulling a red wagon with a delirious little girl in the back. I was in and out of consciousness but awoke when the doctor yelled, "Hospitalization." I learned a new word that day and knew the doctor was disturbed when he asked Linda for our guardian. I remember Linda turning red and shrugging her shoulders as she looked at the emergency room doctor. I lost consciousness again.

I awoke in the children's (and babies) ward of Las Cruces Memorial Hospital. Coincidentally, I was in the same ward where I was born over eight years earlier. I awoke when my mom came to visit me. I remember being upset that Badu came with my mom and not my daddy. The nurses asked for my visitors to leave after seeing me so upset.

"Where was Daddy?" I questioned. Badu should not have come to visit me instead of my daddy. I did not like Badu and let him know that. The nurses saw that I was visibly shaken and tried to calm me. It was the last time I would see them together while I convalesced in the hospital.

I had time to think while I lay in my hospital bed.

Many sad events happened when we moved to Campo Street in Las Cruces after my dad left. Linda and I used to swim in the ditch behind Badu's trailer. One time Linda came out of the ditch with a very bloody knee. She had cut her leg on a piece of tin that was in the ditch. There was a lot of blood as Linda waded to the side and got out of the water. Linda had to get stitches and still has a large, visible scar on the side of her knee.

We would swim regularly in the ditch by Badu's trailer. I remember swimming under the ditch water control gate. It was a sort of lock that controlled the water level. The challenge of swimming under the locks before they closed was thrilling to me. We did not own a TV, and we made our own fun. It was dangerous, but we did not have adult supervision, and no one told us it was dangerous. The locks were on a timer. We knew that and tried to beat the timed closure.

Anyway, I was in the hospital for weeks. I remember the nice nurses gently scolding me for throwing the awful-tasting little workman bottle containing children's liquid vitamins behind my bed. They informed me that the cleaning team would have trouble washing the yellow-orange stains off the wall behind my bed. The kind nurses told me that I should be taking the vitamins to gain my strength and heal quicker. I felt embarrassed that they found out about my daily ritual, but I knew that the nurses were right.

The next visitors I had in the hospital were the child welfare caseworker and Mrs. Gregoria Garcia, my new foster mother. They explained that my sisters were already placed in the Garcia's foster home in Dona Ana, New Mexico. It was a small town nearby. They informed me that I would join my sisters in the foster home as soon as I was well enough. Mrs. Garcia came to see me alone next time.

My foster mom, Mrs. Garcia, seemed like a nice enough lady, but I was a little afraid. I was just relieved that Badu would not be coming to visit anymore. The caseworker explained to me that Mrs. Garcia would check me out of the hospital to go home with her the next time she came to visit. My sisters, her daughter, and little Jo Jo were waiting.

I was confused. Where was Daddy? Surely, he would rescue me from the near-death experience that had landed me in the hospital. Surely, he would find out where was Dona Ana and take me out of the foster home. Surely.

4

Foster Home

Jo Jo ran and was the first person I met at our new home in Dona Ana. Jo Jo was a toddler who was in foster care, too. Jo Jo had two holes in his heart. He returned to his biological mom while we were at the Garcia's and died shortly after his return. I remember playing with Jo Jo. He was a skinny and wiry toddler who was full of joy. I was saddened that he had to go home. I liked Jo Jo and wanted him to stay with us and be my little brother. It was sad to me when I learned he had died years later.

Mrs. Garcia enrolled me in fifth grade at Dona Ana Public Elementary School. It was near our foster home. I remember the fifth grade teacher telling me that I was more advanced than my classmates. I was a November birthday, The cutoff date, at that time, was December 31st. Campbell told me that I would be helping the other fifth graders. I transferred from Catholic School when we moved to Dona Ana. Catholic school had sometimes mean nuns, but they taught us well and eliminated immediately any behavior problems. I thought helping other students learn was cool because I enjoyed helping others.

Alonzo Jackson and his family were the only African Americans at Dona Ana Elementary School. I remember my Hispanic classmates warning me not to play with Alonzo because he would give me "cooties." I thought that comment was very rude. I ignored them, even though I was the new student, and I felt sorry for the Jacksons. They became my friends. I played with them frequently outside at recess and disregarded the warning about "cooties." The Jacksons knew I was their friend.

I was good at sports. I liked to compete. I remember running around the track in fifth and sixth grade. My speed gained me a lot of friends. I remember once having a terrible thigh muscle cramp and having to stop running during a meet. Looking back now, I realize that it was after my vaccine. Since my mom either did not have in her possession or did not transfer my vaccination records to the foster home, I had to get another round of vaccinations. I remember taking yet another sugar cube with the polio vaccine in it.

I also remember the terrible event when Mrs. Garcia took us to the health clinic to get our other vaccines. The nurse (or technician) gave me a shot in the arm. The needle came out of the syringe when she pulled out the shot. She told me not to look, but I did. I saw the needle inserted into my arm with only a small piece hanging out. The nurse told me to hold still as she hooked up another syringe to pull out the hanging needle. I was still, but I do remember the frightening feeling at the sight of the half-inserted needle hanging from my arm.

Mrs. Gregoria Garcia was a good seamstress. She made us dresses to wear to school. We had to wear our dress two days in a row before we could put it in the hamper. We had to change before we completed our daily chores after school. My dress was smelly from the running I did at school. I never sweated a lot but remember changing my dress at the end of the second day.

We learned much at the Garcia's foster home including obedience and discipline. Neither my mom nor my dad ever spanked me. I recall the first real spanking I ever received was with a flyswatter at the Garcia's home.

One day, I learned the meaning of complete obedience. My friends liked to play tetherball with me after school. (My tetherball experience helped to land me on the varsity volleyball team at Mayfield Public High School later as I never attended the right volleyball camps. We could not afford it, and I did not know about them.)

I told my friends one day that they could play tetherball as I completed my chores inside. I was required to complete daily chores after school. I knew the rules. I knew that my friends could not play tetherball without me being present. I disobeyed the rules and remembered Mrs. Garcia asking me to repeat the rules before she swatted my leg with the flyswatter. Mrs. Garcia gave me my first spanking. I did not let my friends play without me being present again. Mrs. Garcia got my attention and taught me a valuable lesson about partial obedience.

We would arise early before school to pick the worms off the tomato plants at the foster home. I enjoyed this early morning activity with Tio (or

Uncle in Spanish) Abelardo. He lived with his brother, Robert, and his wife. Tio never married and did jobs for the Garcias.

In the summer, we would pick cotton and take our bundles to the cotton gin at the corner of our road in Dona Ana. The Garcias harvested three acres of cotton. On the side of the house, we grew sugar cane. I remember how sweet the stalks were. I later found out that the non-nutritional white crystals floated to the top during boiling were to make the non-nutritive white cane sugar.

I celebrated my 11th birthday on November 22, 1963, at our foster home. I walked home early to catch Mrs. Garcia making a birthday cake. I lied and told the school officials that I did not feel good. I just wanted to get home early on my birthday. I was a good student, so the teachers believed me and let me leave early. I walked into the Garcias' to find Mrs. Garcia crying in front of the television, the birthday cake burning.

Our U.S. president, JFK, had been shot in the head while in Dallas. Mrs. Garcia explained that the President was just pronounced dead. She told me of the sad scene when Jacqueline Kennedy, the First Lady, tried to hold on to her husband's head. Mrs. Garcia said that Jacqueline appeared to be trying to gather pieces of her husband's skull. We found out later that she was. That evening was a birthday "celebration" I will never forget.

The Garcias, like my dad, were leery of the Kennedys before he was elected as U.S. president. Mrs. Garcia would talk about what a good president Dwight D. Eisenhower had been. Still, this was the president of the United States who was assassinated in front of all the people watching the open motorcade in Dallas, Texas. It was a very sad birthday.

After two years, Mrs. Garcia gathered us around her to tell my sisters and me that Mom had been rehabilitated. She told us we would have to go back to be with our biological mom. I was disappointed and confused. I liked the routine and discipline we encountered in Dona Ana. I met with the child welfare worker and told her that if my dad was not with my mom, I did not want to go back. (I later found out that Daddy had looked for us while he was on one of his "trips." Zura—the new woman in Daddy's life— told me so.)

Neither the social worker nor the social services would tell Daddy we were placed in a foster home in another town after I was hospitalized. He had abandoned his family and left me to be hospitalized. He was not allowed to know where we were placed in foster care. I did not want to return to Momma. I had learned that my Mom had a baby by Raymundo. Her name was Raymunda, but we quickly changed her name to Sylvia when we returned to Momma. I still resented and disliked Raymundo. He was not my daddy, and I did not want to have even his name in our house. I also learned that Momma was still drinking heavily. My dad hated alcohol, and I was disgusted to learn the truth. I did not want to leave the Garcias' foster home.

5

Ronnie and Vietnam

My mom loved all her children, even those who lived elsewhere. It was the abuse she encountered from relatives that caused her to distort her view of being a wife and mother. She brought it all up later, and I understood her.

We returned to our Momma in the summer of 1964. I was going into seventh grade. I grew to love my little sister, Sylvia. I held her and cared for her as if she was my baby. Momma was very protective of Sylvia, though, and seemed to breastfeed her all the time. My mom loved us all and sacrificed for us all. She later explained to me the dysfunction she had with my dad and why she was unfaithful.

Mom explained with much detail about her first marriage to Gene Hicks, Ronnie's dad, who was a World War II veteran. This was years before she met my dad. My mom and Gene had two children, Ronald Gene and Patricia. Years later my daddy took us to visit Mom's and Gene's son, Ronnie, in Upper Saddle River, NJ. Ronnie was living with his dad's sister, Bonnie Crockett. Ronnie was taken from my mom after Patricia died. Patricia, according to my mom's written account, was a healthy, happy baby one day, and she died the next day. According to my mom, she received her vaccines one day and died the next day. Was there a connection? Who knows as it was not reported nor investigated. We will never know the cause, but my mom still remembers the painful effect of losing a baby.

Gene Hicks went to fight in the Battle of the Bulge in WWII. He was considered a war hero as he fought back Hitler's forces in Belgium, Luxembourg, and France. According to Mom's written account, she was engaged to Gene Hicks when she went to a party and met up with Bill Maes. My oldest sister, Velveeta (or Louise), was conceived that night. Louise, too, was raised with her dad's family. Louise was a kind, accomplished, and good sister. I remember our visits to see her at the Maes' complex on 2nd Street in downtown Albuquerque. Louise was patient and kind. Louise seemed calm, and I respected her. I love my oldest sister who still means so much to me.

Well, Ronnie left his aunt when he was a senior in high school. He came to New Mexico to live with Momma and attended Las Cruces High

School when I was in junior high school at Alameda after I returned from the foster home. He played the drums and was on the wrestling team. He wanted to help in the fight against Communism (and did not have a draft deferment when his draft number came up), so he enlisted in the Marine Corps and went to Vietnam.

Ronnie wrote extensively about his experience in Vietnam. I shared his letters with my Vietnam class when I was getting my master's degree at Converse College in Spartanburg County. We moved back to Greenville County, and I do not know what happened to Ronnie's letters.

Top left and bottom: Louise and sisters.
Top right: Ronnie and sisters.

Ronnie got married to a Vietnamese girl while serving in Vietnam. I do remember Ronnie (and later Mandy Sanchez) write that Vietnam was a confusing war in that it was hard to identify the enemy. The South Vietnamese soldiers and the Viet Cong intermingled. In addition, there was much corruption in the South Vietnamese government. It was hard to know who we were fighting. It was clear to the soldiers that the U.S.A. was fighting the spread of Communism as it was atheistic and totalitarian. The Vietnam War itself was confusing. I know now that it was mismanaged.

While we were living on Alameda Street in Las Cruces, after my brother came to live with us, my mom kept an account at a small grocery store. We all knew it as Don David's. We would "buy" food items and goodies at Don David's and ask for him to put them on our tab. I knew little about settling accounts at the end of the month, but I thought it was cool that we could buy things, ask Don David to write down our purchase on his notepad (making a carbon copy for his records), and pay our account at the end of the month.

We moved to Campo Street in Las Cruces. I made friends with Susie Soto. She introduced us to Vicki Lopez and her brother, Gene. Vicki was very pretty. I thought she had a perfect smile. I had a crush on Vicki's little brother, Gene. I knew that he would be my boyfriend forever as I was in middle school and did not know any better. I did not know it was just puppy love.

It was because of my connection to the Lopez family that I got a job at the local Marquez Tortilla Factory. I started to work by marking the day-old flour tortillas with a black diagonal line but got promoted to the job of using the hot sealing machine to seal the flour tortilla bags. We worked for a few hours after school, and I loved it. I remember Vicki and Linda wearing hair nets as they lined up and rolled flour tortillas. I have great memories of working at the Marquez Tortilla Factory. It was my place to belong shortly after I returned from the foster home. I loved the people with whom I worked.

6

Life in the Projects

My oldest sister, Louise, came to visit us on occasion. She never lived with us, but I loved and respected her. Once when she and her family came to visit in Las Cruces, I begged her to take me to live with her in Albuquerque as I did not like the poverty-laden life and alcoholism of my mom when we lived in Las Cruces. I stayed with Louise for several months but missed my other sisters, so she took me back to Las Cruces.

Louise was good to me when I lived with her. I helped her with her daughters, Laura, Cheryl, and baby Jennifer. When I moved back to Las Cruces, I missed the nieces but knew I needed to be with my mom and sisters in the housing projects. I came home and enrolled at Alameda Junior High School as my mom had moved the family to the housing projects on Locust Street in Las Cruces.

I liked algebra. I had a good teacher. Algebra was like a puzzle to me. In middle school, our schoolwork and homework were our own. Algebra homework was fun for me. I enjoyed the challenge of the puzzle-like questions. Maybe that is why I still love the movie *Hidden Figures* about three mathematical geniuses. I also liked sports. I knew that I had a natural ability in sports, so I tried out for the middle school basketball team.

My classmates and friends knew I would make the team because of my natural skill. After physical education class, I saw the posted roster of who made the team. I was shocked, along with others who saw the roster of team members. I was not on the team roster. It was hard to understand how the girls on the roster made the team ahead of me. It was my first real lesson about money, influence, and politics. I was a poor Hispanic girl from the projects. My mom was not involved in my school activities at all. I knew, at my young age, why I did not make the basketball team. It was a lesson in human nature I will never forget.

Even though we lived in low-income housing projects, honestly, some of my best memories of my teenage years were made while we lived on Locust Street in the housing projects in Las Cruces. My best friend, and later boyfriend, was Mercy Padilla. His sister, Magda, was respected (feared) by those who knew her. Magda was considered a Pachuca (female gang-looking street fighter) who was tiny but fierce. Betty, Mercy's younger sister, was goofy and fun to be with. She looked more African American than Hispanic. Betty and I choreographed a song by Motown artists and won the Shina Baloo (local dance contest) at our local community center two years in a row. One year, we won the contest as we choreographed and danced to *Tracks of My Tears* by Smokey Robinson.

The "project gang," as we were known, included Patsy and Paul Padilla, Mercy, Magda, Betty, Terry, and Terry's brother, Melito. My sister, Linda, and I were also in the gang. We would play ball (not unlike *The Sandlot* movie) during the hot summer days. I, then, would follow Mercy to his Little League and Connie Mack baseball games. At night, we would play dogpile.

The object of dogpile was to chase a boy or girl (either one) and, if we caught a person, wrestle them to the ground and yell, "Dogpile!" It was like modified football with no pads and was played with a mix of boys and girls. It was dangerous, but we had so much fun chasing and tackling each other. Mercy called out Melito because of the roughness of the game. They got into a terrible fight because of the game and other reasons. That incident was the only sad memory I have of living in the projects.

During certain seasons, I would walk home from middle school. It was about two miles from school to the projects. I could ride the bus, but I liked waiting for the athletes who practiced after school. Stevie Pettis was one of the athletes. He was my friend, and I liked walking home with him. Mercy was another with whom I walked. He was a disciplined athlete and scholar. I admired and respected him very much.

When Mercy met and started dating the girl from Las Cruces High after we broke up after middle school, it hurt me, but I never told anyone. Mercy ended up marrying her although he escorted me when I won Senior Winter Ball Princess at Mayfield High School. I had a shocked reaction when I heard my name being called over the intercom speaker at the large public high school. I was a poor Hispanic, and my parents were not volunteers. Why would I be voted to receive this honor by my classmates? I was from a broken home and had no influence. I was startled, but it happened. I won for the princess. How was this poor Hispanic girl going to be a princess of a large public high school where only wealthy people had status? I was shocked but honored. I had no family members there to honor me. I was used to not having a support system.

Mercy told me the above when he escorted me to the Winter Ball. We were not an item, but I knew he cared for me, so I asked him to escort me for this honor. He was concerned about me while I was in high school because of my friends, including Barbara Gomez — who was wealthy, lived in a big house, and whose dad was in county government. Barbara held wild parties on the weekends. I dismissed his criticism in anger. I never saw Mercy Padilla again.

7

Where Have All the Good Men Gone?

I begged my sister, Louise, to take me to live with her twice when she came to visit us—once while I was in junior high and once while I was in high school. My unhappiness in the projects was because of several events. First, I wanted my daddy to come back. I cried for him nightly and believed he was dead, in prison, or had amnesia. I knew he would not be gone from his girls if he could help it. Daddy loved me, and he was my friend.

My mom only had good things to say about daddy. It was a mystery to me that he left without a trace and had not contacted us. I knew he must be dead. I also felt shame because of all the above and was distant from my mom who spent all her time devoted to Sylvia. She was a good momma and was nurturing and loving. As a teenager, however, I needed structure and discipline. My mom did not provide either. I was unhappy and wanted to leave the projects.

Louise agreed to take me to live with her family in Albuquerque again. While I lived with Louise near Winrock Mall in Northeast Heights, I attended Sandia High School. Louise and her husband, Daryl Petrig, had recently returned from Germany. Jennifer, their third daughter, had been diagnosed with leukemia, so they received a compassionate transfer to return to Albuquerque for treatment. Jennifer died April 24, 1966. Jennifer was Daryl's only biological daughter. Louise had two daughters from a prior marriage. Daryl was devoted to them while married to my oldest sister.

I was keenly interested and aware of current events even though I watched little TV. I enjoyed reading the newspaper though. Two tragic deaths happened while I was in Albuquerque in 1968. One was the assassination of Martin Luther King Jr. I admired Dr. King. I applauded his nonviolent stance in the face of violent opposition. I did not like the extremism of Malcolm X. His ways would produce resistance to his violent rebellion. Malcolm X and Martin Luther King Jr. had different visions to change America. There was racism because that is human nature. There has *always* been racism whether it was the Egyptians discriminating against the Hebrews, the Apache Indians fighting the peaceable Pueblo Indians, the Germans discriminating against the Jews, the Japanese discriminating against the Chinese, or tribal warfare in Africa. It is human nature.

Martin Luther King Jr. sought to end racist acts against Southern Democrats. Dr. King was well educated. He graduated from Morehouse College when he was 19 years old. He was a smart man and knew human nature. He was wise. The people threatened by his message opposed him. He was martyred as was Christ. Dr. King taught that Christ suffered and died for humans. MLK Jr did too. Humans change when they experience sacrifice for others.

King changed the political climate in America. He achieved the Civil Rights legislation. Hearts and human nature, however, can never be changed permanently without being born again with a new set of values. I honor the Reverend Dr. Martin Luther King Jr. today. (Coincidentally, I write this section on the day the U.S.A. celebrates MLK Jr.)

Malcom X was also shot and martyred. He sought change through violence, however. MLK Jr. once said about Malcolm X,

> Fiery, demagogic oratory in the Black ghettos, urging Negroes to arm themselves and prepare to engage in violence, as he has done, can reap nothing but grief.[3]

Dr. King was right. We do not celebrate the life of Malcolm X.

I remember the later slain Robert F. Kennedy's spontaneous speech in the bed of a truck when he learned of MLK Jr's assassination. RFK urged compassion and a change of heart. He quoted the ancient Greek poet, Aeschylus. He delivered a speech from the back of a truck shortly after King was assassinated in Memphis and said,

> My favorite poet was Aeschylus. He once wrote, "And even in our sleep, pain which cannot forget falls drop by drop upon

the heart, until in our own despair, against our will, comes wisdom through the awful grace of God."[4]

Kennedy was slain that same year as Dr. King.

Palestinian-born Sirhan Sirhan needed a heart change. Yet, he took the life of RFK and shot many others in Los Angeles, California. At a presidential campaign stop, Sirhan took the life of a civil rights political advocate who worked tirelessly to fight racism and Communism. I grieved their assassinations during the summer of 1968. My longing to travel back to Las Cruces increased because of their sudden deaths and for other reasons.

I wanted to return to Las Cruces soon. I missed my sisters and was concerned about them. I also wanted to return because of the trouble I got into with my sister, Louise, and brother-in-law, Daryl.

I loved soul music. When my friends asked for me to take them to hear James Brown at his stop in Albuquerque on his way to Oklahoma during his 1968 "There Was a Time" tour, it was a no-brainer. Of course, I would take them. I agreed to take my friends in my sister's blue station wagon. Daryl and Louise had gone out for the evening. The car had a column shift, but I was a good driver like my sister, Linda. After all, I was 14 now and had my learner's permit. I would get my New Mexico driver's license in a few months, and I knew how to drive a standard shift transmission. It was hard for me to understand why my sister and her husband were so angry when we returned. I was scolded and grounded. This punishment probably led me to want to return to Las Cruces where my mom had no rules for us to follow.

When I returned to Las Cruces the first time, Linda was dating a guy by the name of Richard. He was a good man and was determined to date Linda. Richard was persistent and knew Linda was the only one for him. So, he waited and tolerated. He was, and still is, a patient, kind, and generous man. I pondered why outgoing Linda spent so much time with shy Richard, but I grew to love Richard and his family. They were and are wonderful human beings.

Richard was a great outdoorsman and hunter. Richard was reserved but very accomplished. He was a very fast runner and a great athlete at Las Cruces High. He was on the track and football teams. I was protective of my sister and saw that she was falling for him. I cried when she eventually married Richard. I did not want to lose my big sister. She finished high school while married and lived with Richard's mom. Fifty-six years later Linda is still married to Richard.

Richard was and still is a big part of our family. We all grew to love him. When I was in middle school, Richard took us for joyrides in his old Jeep. We would tell our friends we were going "boondocking" after school and invited others to join us. Boondocking was when several teenagers piled into a vehicle and went for a bumpy off-the-road ride. We did not have an off-the-road vehicle, so we went in Richard's old Jeep. We took a friend, named Lupe, on one of our trips.

We were bouncing over numerous creosote and mesquite bushes on the Llano, east of Locust Court, where we lived in the housing projects. At that time, the I-25 interstate highway was nonexistent. We were romping around the Llano with a Jeep-load full of fun pleasure-seekers, and I guess Lupe forgot to hold on for one of the airborne experiences, and it was then that she banged her head on the sliding glass window on the left side of the Jeep behind the driver's seat. She did get banged up, but the Jeep's window only cracked. The window was harder than Lupe's head, I guess.

Another time, we got into trouble on a very late school night. We went on a joyride. Richard was the driver of his jeep and recalled the night.

"We took off on a deep arroyo behind Mesilla Dam. We high-centered as we drove off the road when we finally contacted earth, and luckily the turtle shell under the Willys offered protection to the transmission and drive train. We were able to dig out and decided it was time to head home and face the music [with my mom and his parents]," said Richard.

He was right. We had to explain to my mom why we came home at 2:00 a.m. on a school night. We knew it was going to be a long night as we explained the details to my mom before he left.

Richard and Linda dated for years and eventually got married during the summer between Linda's junior and senior years in high school. It was not unusual to get married young in the Hispanic culture. Richard was going into the service as he was a few years older than Linda. I cried at their wedding as I felt I was losing my protector. My dad was gone, and I looked to Linda and Louise for my protection. Now Louise and Linda would both be married.

Linda lived with her in-laws during her senior year. Elisa Enriquez was a good, godly lady. Elisa even made dresses for me and my sisters to wear to Linda and Richard's wedding. Elisa taught Linda how to sew and cook while Richard served in the Air Force. Richard was assigned to unload body bags on the west coast. The body bag count became the measure of success during the Vietnam War.

After Linda left to live with Richard's family, I went to work as a car-hop at the Topper Restaurant. The Topper, outside Las Cruces, carries many good memories. I worked there as a junior in high school. I did my homework when not waiting on cars outside. I made good tips and worked with great people. I loved my job. I was introduced to drag racing as the Topper Restaurant sponsored a stock car and produced a stock car queen. I enjoyed watching the cars race and was excited that I was friends with a queen.

One late Saturday night, I looked out the serving window and saw someone who looked like Johnny Cash, the "Man in Black." My friends at the Topper laughed at me and made fun of my thought. "Sure," they said. "We dare you to go out to the dining area and ask him if he is Johnny Cash." They did not really expect me to go out, but I took off my apron, and I did.

Johnny Cash was sitting with two women. He was sitting with Carrie Rivers and June Carter Cash (his mother and second wife respectively). When I asked, "Excuse me, sir, but by any chance could you be Johnny Cash?"

He smiled that sheepish smile and replied with a slight accent, "Yes, ma'am. I am."

I looked at my friends with a smile as they were staring at me out of the window. Then I asked for Johnny Cash's autograph. He tore off a piece of the placemat and signed it. I then asked shyly why he was eating at the Topper. He replied that he had performed in El Paso, Texas, that night and was on his way home. (El Paso was about thirty miles south of Las Cruces). Cash, his mom, and his wife were warm and friendly. I scurried back to the kitchen and felt proud that I was brave enough to venture out and confirm my speculation.

High school was demanding as a junior even though I was not on the college track. I had asked my high school guidance counselor if I should take courses on the college track. He looked surprised at me and replied in a matter-of-fact tone, "Poor Hispanic women do not go to college! They get married and have babies."

Okay, then, I thought. College was out for me. After all, nobody in my family had gone to college.

I remembered those words when I received my bachelor's degree, master's degree, and was awarded the annual James Madison Memorial Fellowship Foundation Scholarship—awarded to one teacher per state per year. Poor Hispanic girls could achieve. I was motivated to achieve good grades in college partially because of my high school counselor's words. He motivated me with his negative words. I was determined to prove him wrong. Hispanic women could do more than get married and have babies.

The next year as a senior in high school, I tried out and made the varsity volleyball team. I remember the fun of practice and traveling with the team. There was something that I wanted, however. I wanted a car. We were poor, and I would have to work to buy a car. I wanted to drive. I knew I could not play sports and go to practice and have a job too.

When it was announced during morning announcements that White Sands Missile Range was looking for high school seniors to work part-time, I knew it was for me. I applied for a job.

When I was notified that I was approved for the program, I had to tell my volleyball coach that I was going to quit the team. I do not remember much about the encounter but felt confident I made the right decision. After all, I was elected treasurer of the Office Education Association and had much homework to complete instead of practicing and traveling with the team. Since then, however, I have sometimes regretted not being pictured with the varsity volleyball team at Mayfield High.

8

Joseph Herring

Ohne man changed my life's trajectory when I was a high school senior. His name was Mr. Joseph Herring.

Mr. Joseph Herring was the Equal Employment Opportunity Officer (EEO) at White Sands Missile Range. He was my boss. I worked in his office when I was hired part-time as a senior in high school. He had a secretary named Margaret, and I would work with her. Mr. Herring was a large man. He was a nice man. He reminded me of Hoss on *Bonanza*—the only Sunday night TV show we were allowed to watch while at the Garcias' foster home.

Shortly after I started to work for Mr. Herring, he asked the question, "Where are you going to college next year?"

I was embarrassed but replied honestly that I was not going to college. I repeated what my high school counselor had reminded me. I told Mr. Herring that I thought about going to a two-year technical school but had not made plans.

"Why aren't you going to college?" Mr. Herring asked.

"I am not on the college track," I replied.

"Why don't you take college prep courses?" Mr. Herring continued.

I had to be honest and tell him about the conversation I had with my guidance counselor when I was a sophomore.

"Hispanic girls get married and have babies," I sheepishly replied.

Mr. Herring said, "Baloney," (or another "b" word) when I told him that "poor Hispanic girls got married and had babies. They do not go to college."

Mr. Herring was appalled when I told him that my guidance counselor was Hispanic, too. (I was technically half Hispanic but considered myself Hispanic because I looked Hispanic, was bilingual, and my mom and friends were Hispanic.)

He then asked, "What is your score on the college entrance exam?"

I replied that I had not taken one. He was persistent and asked, "Why have you not taken the exam?"

I told Mr. Herring, "It costs money to register for the entrance exam. I don't have the money."

Mr. Herring then said, "I will pay for it. When is the next one scheduled?"

When I replied that I did not follow the dates, he said that he would find out. I told him that we still had a problem.

"I am working to pay for a car. I did not have a ride to take the exam." Mr. Herring replied that he would find the date, pay for the exam, and drive me to take it. Mr. Herring was not going to accept my excuses and insisted on taking me to the college entrance exam!

Mr. Herring waited anxiously for my exam scores. He asked me for them daily when I was at work. When the scores finally arrived, I took them to him the next day. He sat back in his chair after I showed the scores to him, and he proudly announced with a smile, "You can attend any state school with these scores!" While I was pleased with his response, I still had a problem.

"I have no money to pay for tuition," I told him.

He again replied with assurance. "Then I will find a federal program for you! You are going to college!"

I knew at this point that it was futile to argue with Mr. Herring. I was, frankly, surprised that he took such an interest and acted on behalf of a young Hispanic female employee. He was a good man who sincerely cared.

Mr. Herring was not fully appreciated until years later when I reflected on what he did for me. I resigned myself to taking his guidance and his advice. Mr. Herring did find a federal program and helped me with the application process.

Needless to say, Mr. Joseph Herring changed my life. He was a model mentor and friend. His happiness came from helping others. He was an exceptional human being, and I owe any successes I have had professionally to Mr. Herring. I loved college and received good grades for my bachelor's and my master's degrees in education. Mr. Herring was an encourager. He saw the hidden talents that no one else saw. He made me believe in myself.

Mr. Herring impacted my life in many ways while I was a senior in high school. He encouraged me to write an administrative manual for office workers. I wrote the manual and joined the Office Education Association (OEA). I entered the manual in the state competition at the annual OEA conference. Mrs. Della Taylor was the OEA high school sponsor.

Mayfield High School Yearbook (Shield '70)
Las Cruces Sun-News; *White Sands Missile Range*
Newspaper Archive (1969-1970)

Mrs. Taylor sat across from me when the OEA state winners were announced. The first place winner went to the person expected and primed to win. She was the president of our Mayfield Club and was very skilled at writing. Mrs. Taylor turned white and almost fell back when my name was called as the state second place winner. I was even surprised at the victory. But Mr. Herring wasn't. He told me I had the gift of writing, which was why he encouraged me to write an office manual. He was right again.

Mr. Herring believed in me. He is responsible for the academic and social successes I had as a senior in high school and a freshman in college. I won for princess and queen. He believed I could do anything I set my mind to do. Everyone needs an encourager. My dad, Linda, and Louise were gone. Mr. Herring was sent as an angel to guide and encourage me.

9

NMSU, UNM, and EDPA

True to his word, Mr. Herring found a federal program whereby if I taught in a low-income, largely Hispanic bilingual program during the day as a teacher's aide, I would receive full-time college tuition and could attend night classes as a full-time student.

Maybe it was because I never expected to go. Maybe it was because I loved learning. I do not know the reason, but I loved college!

My first class at New Mexico State University (NMSU) started at 6:40 a.m. and ended at 7:30 a. m. in time for me to drive to Hermosa Heights Elementary School where I worked as a teacher's aide in first grade.

Mrs. Rodney was the first grade teacher I assisted until she took maternity leave in December. I learned so much from this master teacher. Mrs. Rodney modeled efficiency and compassion. I watched her in awe. She genuinely loved the mostly Hispanic and bilingual students in her classroom. When she left at Christmas due to her advanced pregnancy, I worked with a teacher who had not been in the classroom for years. Since I knew the students and their routine, she gave me much authority in the classroom. I was only 18 but picked up the skill of teaching quickly. I loved it.

Schoolwork ended for me at 4:00 p.m. I ate dinner and returned for my evening classes to be a full-time student. I lived with the Armendariz family during my freshman year of college. They were a wonderful couple, and Mr. Jose Armendariz worked as an electrician at White Sands Missile Range (WSMR). I awoke with him early to go to class and for him to catch and ride the bus over the Oregon Mountains. I loved our morning chats. I also learned to drink rich black coffee. The coffee kept me going that year as I juggled college, work, and homework. I loved college. Not knowing what to declare, I was a business education major at NMSU because of the influence of Mr. Herring. It was a crazy schedule as I juggled school and college, but I received good grades, and I loved it.

During the summer of 1971, my friends from Northern New Mexico convinced me to change my major to education and transfer to the University of New Mexico (UNM) in Albuquerque.

I transferred to UNM. It had a great elementary education program. I found a federal program that allowed me to work as the program paid for my tuition. It was different in that it paid part-time tuition, not full-time.

Louise, my older sister, allowed me to live with her while I went to college at UNM. Louise was an encourager who was proud of me for going to college. I was the first one in our family to attend university.

The federal program at UNM was called EDPA-PPS. This federal program allowed Hispanic guidance counselor candidates to get their master's degree and return to counseling, mainly in California's public schools. This program was granted funds by the federal government to help Hispanics.

My middle school friend, Patsy Padilla, was in Albuquerque attending Albuquerque Technical Vocational School (ATVI) for two years. We agreed to rent a house together near both our schools. I walked to UNM, and she drove to ATVI. We both enjoyed our freedom and never had an argument. Patsy eventually got her certificate, married her longtime boyfriend, Tony, and moved back to Las Cruces. I moved in with Ciria.

At a retreat for the EPDA-PPS project, the militant Hispanic guidance counselor candidates (who insisted that we wear brown armbands to signify our unity with the Chicano Power Movement) decided they could run the EPDA-PPS Program better than the administrators. They took control of the program, and we all resigned. The staff knew they could not appease these militants.

I was left abandoned. I had no school tuition. I felt alone again. My dad was still gone on one of his "trips." I longed for his words of affirmation for what I achieved. I cried nightly for his return and knew that he either had amnesia, was imprisoned, or he was dead. I knew that he would not leave and stay gone from his "I baby" if he could help it. I just knew it, but I still felt alone and abandoned.

There was a Marine named David, who had kept in touch with me by letters after I met him when I worked at the Topper Restaurant. I had written to him. He swore that one day he would marry me. I dismissed his promise but had a soft spot for Marines.

My half-brother, Ronnie, was a Marine, and many of my high school and college friends volunteered for the Marines or Navy. Many of them served in Vietnam. Looking back and analyzing the "war" as it was called, I understood the confusion about the times. (It wasn't really a war. Congress passed the Tonkin Gulf Resolution that sent U.S. soldiers to fight and die. That was the only legal justification for the "war.") The Vietnam "War" was different and confusing to those who fought and returned.

The Vietnam War, or McNamara's War as it was also known, was going on during this period of my life. It was a hot spot in the Cold War. I understood the college protests. (The Kent State massacre happened at the end of my senior year in high school.) It was a time of hatred, mistrust, and division. While I understood the mistrust, I also knew the patriotism of those who volunteered to fight the spread of Communism in the Cold War. It was a time of confusion and contradictions. I was caught in this confusing time.

Once I meandered into an anti-war riot. I was at UNM but traveled home to Las Cruces on weekends to see family who lived three hours south in Las Cruces. On one of my Sunday night trips back to UNM, I listened to Santana on my 8-track player while driving for hours. The radio had been off during the entire journey as I listened to Santana's "Oye Como Vay" over and over again.

When I entered Albuquerque from Highway 25 at about 10:00 p.m., I noticed that the streets were empty. It was an eerie feeling, and I knew something was happening. I was familiar with the UFO hysteria coming from Roswell, NM, but this was different. I decided to eject Santana and turn on the radio to find out what was going on in Albuquerque.

There was a curfew called by officials because of the anti-war riots taking place at Roosevelt Park. I was very curious. So instead of going home to a safe location and obeying the curfew mandate, my curiosity took over, and I went to Roosevelt Park to see for myself.

What I saw still gives me chills. Roosevelt Park had many one-way streets. Once I was committed to driving to the top of one of the hills, I could not turn around easily until I reached the top. I entered the one-way street and drove to the top.

There were police cars overturned and on fire. I tried to escape but could not turn around my small Toyota. When an officer ran towards me with tear gas, I quickly rolled up my window. I felt the sting as the tear gas penetrated the window seal. My eyes were stinging, and I wanted out.

The student-protestors were still throwing Molotov cocktails at the police cars. I assumed that was why they were burning. I assumed that was why the policeman came toward me with tear gas. I was a young student, I had a UNM parking sticker on my car, and the policeman assumed I was there to join the riot. He did not know that I was just curious and had driven to the park to find out why there was a curfew. I wanted out of the mess.

Needless to say, it was a long night before we were allowed to leave. I answered several questions correctly, so I was allowed to drive home and not taken to jail like several others.

That night still haunts me. Policemen were our protection. Yet their patrol cars were upside down and burning. I was puzzled that the police would confuse me for an anti-war protestor. I had too many friends who were fighting and dying and were emotional wrecks as a result of Vietnam. No. I was not a protestor.

In my opinion, then and now, the Vietnam War protestors who sat in front of UNM and shouted, "Baby-killers!" to my returning friends were spoiled, rich hippie brats. To be honest, I hated the hippie anti-war movement. I believed many were rich dopeheads who could afford to protest the war while my Hispanic friends were dying and being injured for a cause. They believed they were fighting Communism.

I was not very religious at this time, but I knew atheism was wrong. I believed there was a God. Communism was an atheistic form of government. The Vietnam "War" was a hot spot during the Cold War when two ideologies collided. One ideology was about freedom and a belief in God. The other was about government control and atheism. My friends fought what was later called "evil" by President Ronald Reagan when he referenced a Communist country.

The Vietnam War was fought to stop the domino theory from becoming a reality. The domino theory held the belief that if one Southeast Asian country fell to Communism, others would fall like dominos. It was hard for me to reconcile the hippie/student protests when many had come from a life of luxury. Many were not poor or a minority. Many did not realize that President Eisenhower, then Kennedy and Johnson sent advisors and ultimately escalated the war. Many did not realize that the "war" was being conducted like a business—with victory and loss measured in body-bag counts. The Vietnam War was confusing in many ways.

It was a confusing war, but I knew why soldiers, Marines like my half-brother, enlisted. They enlisted to find a purpose and to fight evil. Little did they know they would face scorn upon their return from those I considered to be privileged, spoiled brats.

No, I was not at Roosevelt Park to protest the war as a college student, but I learned much that night. The Vietnam War and the anti-war protestors left a scar on me. They fought for their ideology. Couldn't protestors understand that soldiers were fighting an ideology that was atheistic?

I felt as though my life was falling apart. David Guzman, a Marine, had pursued me and promised to marry me. I agreed to join him at Camp Lejeune Marine Corps Base where he was stationed as a Military Policeman. Eventually, we married in Las Cruces and returned to Albuquerque.

I was a Catholic and believed that if you live with someone, you should marry that person. During our marriage ceremony, I closed my eyes and asked God not to bless our union. We followed tradition and had a big celebration. I do think God heard my prayer. My marriage was not blessed.

I returned to Albuquerque as a married woman. David served his time as a Marine and attended the University of Albuquerque as he planned to be a policeman. We rented the apartment behind Ciria's apartment on Cornell Street in Albuquerque near UNM.

10

Daddy and D.C.

I **walked to UNM to finish school. It was there during my senior** year of college that I received a shocking phone call. I remember the phone call clearly as I could not believe the man's voice on the other end.

"I baby, I baby," said the man's voice to utter silence on my end. My mind was swarming with thoughts. My heart was swarming with emotions. There was only one person who called me "I baby."

"Daddy?" I finally replied.

His voice was joyful but still with the familiar Southern drawl.

"Yes. It's Daddy." he said. "I have come back. I am in Las Cruces."

Before he could say anymore, I said, "I want to see you. I will drive down to Las Cruces."

As I drove to Las Cruces that day, my mind was swirling with thoughts. It was 11 long years since he left on one of his "trips."

Where had Daddy been for those years?

Did he have amnesia?

Was he in prison?

Then my emotions turned to bitterness and hate.

Where was he when I won second place in New Mexico's State Office Education Conference for writing an office manual in the state in 1969?

Where was he when I was crowned Mayfield High School's Winter Ball Princess? Did Daddy know I walked alone and was not escorted like my friends whose dads escorted them?

Did Daddy know that I was nominated by friends in a large public high school, and I was considered a poor Hispanic?

Where was Daddy when I won for Pan-American Queen in 1970?

I was crowned by the New Mexican Lt. Governor during the annual fiesta in Mesilla, New Mexico.

Did Daddy know that I walked alone in Mesilla and did not have family members to celebrate my victory with me?

Anger and bitterness at Daddy's absence were consuming me when I finally arrived in Las Cruces.

Did Daddy know I cried myself to sleep knowing that he could not return to me? Did Daddy know he broke my heart?

I was reintroduced to my dad. Then I found out the truth. Daddy had met a nurse named Zura. Zura had a daughter named Sandy, and Zura and Daddy had two sons together. One was a Down syndrome child named Jimmy, and the other one was named Jay Scott.

Zura was a nice lady. I could understand why she followed my dad. She told me that Daddy never forgot his three daughters. She told me that he would mention us on our birthdays. Zura tried to blend our families.

As mentioned, Zura was a nice lady. What I couldn't understand was that the dad I cried for nightly, the dad who had given so much to my mom's Catholic religion, the dad who I knew loved me could leave me for another family. It was easier for my sisters to accept Zura, Jimmy, Jay Scott, and Sandy, Zura's other daughter. It was hard for me to accept and to understand.

David and I were together a little over a year. He finished his obligations to the Marines. He was a security guard while he was in school and eventually became a policeman. His friend on the police force was married to a nice Christian lady whose dad was a well-known policeman in another city. I will call them Walter and Catherine.

Walt invited David to join him on his nightly adventures. I suspected David was seeing other women after his night shift as he came home very late. I could not prove it until I saw Walt and David with two women in a car. David had taken off his wedding band, and I knew something was going on. I left him at that point.

It was while I was teaching that I wrote my divorce papers with the help of a lawyer friend. I listed "incompatible" as the reason for wanting a divorce after a little over a year of marriage. The real reason was infidelity. I knew I could never accept someone who was unfaithful.

David said something derogatory about my mom, and that was all I needed to file for a divorce. The judge saw it my way and granted the uncontested filing. The divorce was final less than two years after my dad walked me down the aisle.

I graduated from UNM and worked for the Albuquerque School System (APS) at Emerson Elementary School. My principal, Mr. Mitchell, saw leadership potential in me and asked for me to be the kindergarten department chair. I loved teaching and learned much from my UNM professors and from Ms. Dorella Parella. Ms. Dorella was my supervising teacher when I completed my student teaching at East San Jose Elementary School

Teaching at Emerson was demanding but fulfilling. There was an abundance of teachers available upon graduation from college, and they were looking for work. My teacher's aide was named Cindy, and she had a teaching degree and was certified but could only find a job as a teacher's aide for APS.

There were 25 students in my morning kindergarten and 23 in the afternoon. Most students were minorities and bilingual. Wanting to be an excellent teacher, I met the students at home the summer before school started. Most had never been in a school setting, and many did not speak English. I wanted to develop trust as their new teacher.

I went to one student's home twice. Her name was Stephanie. Her house was near the school in SE Albuquerque, and I went to meet her at her home after I sent a small card to introduce myself.

No one was home when I came the first time. The family had assured me they would be there in writing. Once, while I was in the vicinity visiting another student, I saw a small girl playing outside in Stephanie's yard. I approached her and asked if she was Stephanie.

She looked startled, but replied, "Si. Yo soy Stephanie."

I told her who I was and asked if we could go inside to meet her family.

As soon as we approached her duplex, I inhaled a whiff of the marijuana that was being smoked by Stephanie's mom. Her mom came out to meet me, and we briefly chatted after I introduced myself. I then knew why Stephanie was hungry when she came to kindergarten in the afternoon. I also learned why she fell asleep often. Maybe I should have reported her family immediately. Maybe I had too much compassion for the children whose parents victimized them. Maybe my past caused me to give too much grace. I do not know the reason. I still remember Stephanie, though.

Another student named Jason met me at the back door daily at 7:00 a.m. I got to school early to work before the students arrived. I had developed a habit of rising very early to do schoolwork while in college. When I graduated, I kept this early-to-bed, early-to-rise habit. I arrived at school at 7:00 am. Jason's mom had to be at work at 7:30, so she dropped him off for a free breakfast given to low-income students. There were many students who would eat a free breakfast. They stayed and ate a free lunch before they went home, too. I had the impression that they only ate the two free meals daily. I do not know what they ate on the weekends, holidays, and summers. It was while I was preparing to return to teaching school at Emerson Elementary that my life changed, again.

Ciria had accepted an offer to work in Washington, DC. She called for me to visit her in DC during my summer break. I accepted the offer and flew to Washington, DC during the summer of 1976. Ciria was working for the Office of Bilingual Education (OBE) within the Department of Health, Education, and Welfare. (Education did not become a separate department until 1979.)

Ciria was a program manager, and I visited her office frequently during that summer. I was a teacher in a bilingual elementary school and was curious about the federal program created by the 1968 Bilingual Education Act (BEA). I wanted to learn about the federal government.

What I encountered that summer helped form my views about government programs. I found that program writers and administrators came in late, took long lunches, and left early. When they did work, regulations were written for local teachers and coordinators to complete. I was a conscientious teacher. I would teach all day and complete the forms at night to make sure we were meeting needs as prescribed by the federal government.

By the end of the summer in DC, Ciria urged me to apply for a job being vacated by a lawyer friend on Capitol Hill. I did. I was reluctant because I was not a lawyer, but they were looking to hire a bilingual educator. Ciria encouraged me to apply for the experience.

Congressman Herman Badillo was a bilingual and the first Puerto Rican U.S. Congressman representing the South Bronx in New York City. Our interview went well, and he offered me the job at the end. There was a dilemma, however. I had already signed a contract with APS to return to teach kindergarten at Emerson Elementary. I called my principal.

Mr. Mitchell, my principal, was nice and he was encouraging. He said basically that my job would be waiting for me when I returned from a once-in-a-lifetime opportunity to work on Capitol Hill as a staffer. He said he would offer my teaching job to Cindy, my aide, since she had a teaching degree and knew the school and classroom routine. I offered her all of the handmade teaching props that I made while in college. I did not see Cindy nor any of my teaching materials again. I never returned to live in New Mexico. There was a hand guiding me, but I did not know it at the time.

11

Capitol Hill

Working for U.S. Congressman Herman Badillo was exciting, educational, and exhausting. I was determined to succeed. It was hard to believe that this poor Hispanic girl from New Mexico was offered a job on Capitol Hill working for a U.S. Congressman representing the South Bronx of New York.

When I worked for Congressman Badillo, his staff was invited to meet President Gerald Ford as part of the National Hispanic Heritage celebration. I went as a representative of Congressman Herman Badillo. I met President Ford in one of the colored rooms in the White House. President Ford seemed to be a genuinely nice person. He shook my hand and told me about his work for Hispanics. It was hard to believe I was actually talking to the president of the United States.

President Ford had received much criticism from mostly Democrats for pardoning former president Richard M. Nixon after Nixon resigned from the presidency. Nixon's resignation was a result of his taped conversations and his cover-up. It was not just due to the spying at the Watergate Hotel to discover plans by the Democrats to elect George McGovern in 1972. It was the cover-up that cost him his job. President Ford had assumed the vice presidency after Vice President Spiro Agnew resigned. He resisted the cry to prosecute Nixon to avoid further political division.

My political and philosophical ideology was largely set during these years working on the Hill. I worked for Congressman Badillo in the Cannon House Office Building. I learned a lot, but the learning curve was steep and very high. I was a hard worker and was determined to succeed.

My desk was in Mira's office. Mira was the congressman's administrative assistant (AA). She liked me, and we would chat when she wasn't reading the New York papers. Outside our office sat Cesarina. She was the receptionist in the congressman's office. Cesarina's dad was a translator at the United Nations in New York City. Cesarina's family came from Cuba, and we became fast friends. She was rather aristocratic, and I was not, but we enjoyed each other, and I traveled with Cesarina to New York City to meet her family and tour the South Bronx.

One lunch hour, I was sitting in my office working when I heard a man's voice in the reception area. The man asked Cesarina whose initials were I.R.. I had unofficially changed my name back to my maiden name, Idell Revell. He said that he knew the congressman had not written a reply to his request for endorsement from the congressman to obtain federal funds. He claimed that I.R. was going to be responsible for the congressman's reelection bid failure. I overheard this threat to my friend.

Cesarina should not face this hostility alone, I thought. I had done the research and written the response to Mr. Ed Blankenstein representing Tri-County Technical School in the South Bronx. Tri-County Tech did not qualify for federal funds per the regulations written, which I had read. I wrote that fact in my reply that had Congressman Badillo's signature.

Mr. Blankenstein's lawyer and Mr. Blankenstein were big men. I came out to rescue Cesarina, extended my hand, and said, "I am I.R What can I do for you?" I invited them to chat in the congressman's office. I suppose Cesarina went to get the congressman as she left right after we entered the office. I was a little public school teacher and was unprepared for the high stakes of the political world. (I would later teach a political workshop titled "Blood Sport: American Politics." I thought of my encounter that day in the congressman's office when I titled the course.)

I calmly explained that I read the federal regulations. His technical school did not qualify according to the written regulations, and the congressman could not endorse him as his school did not qualify for federal funds. I was told, with a big finger pointing at me, that I would be responsible for the congressman's defeat in his re-election bid and that Mr. Blankenstein, his lawyer, and others would make sure he was defeated. I knew the congressman would not violate the rules for politics. I was terrified that I messed up. I was shaking, and I doubted my research. I would not change my recommendation, however. They left in anger.

When the congressman finally returned, I was an emotional wreck. I explained what happened. The congressman was kind and gracious but said I should not have confronted the men alone. He also advised me to communicate with the New York delegation which I did.

After talking to several other staffers and the legislative aide to U.S. Senator Edward "Ted" Kennedy, I found out that I was right. Mr. Blankenstein's school did not qualify. I was told that he was endorsed annually because no one took the time to compare the regulations with his application. I was assured that I was doing what was right. I was told that the congressional delegation would write to Mr. Blankenstein and tell him that he didn't qualify. We never heard from Mr. Blankenstein nor his lawyer again. Congressman Herman Badillo won re-election and even ran for mayor of New York City.

In DC, I ran into culture shock as well. In New Mexico, I knew mostly Hispanics. I considered myself Hispanic because I looked like my mom. My daddy was not Hispanic. My closest friend in Washington, DC was the night clerk at Ciria's high-rise apartment complex. His name was Azu. He was from Nigeria, Africa, and was studying at Georgetown. I met Azu as soon as I moved to DC. Ciria spent a lot of time with her boyfriend, Ed. Azu took me under his wing and tried to teach me the pitfalls of a large, international political city. Azu and I played tennis often or went out to eat. I felt safe with this tall, lanky black man.

I learned from Azu why it was necessary to activate the large wooden parking arm with my parking card. I learned from Azu why, after I went around the horseshoe when the large arm let me in, I would have to use another card to open the garage door. I learned from Azu that after entering the parking garage and parking a car, I had to use a special key to get into the elevator. I then had to use another key to unlock the deadbolt lock to enter the apartment. I learned that still another key was required to turn off the alarm system. All these steps were necessary, I learned from Azu, because the crime rate was so high.

Azu had learned much and taught me much about the high crime in DC. DC was much different from New Mexico. It was truly a culture shock. There was crime in New Mexico as human nature is the same. However, it was not as visible as it was in our nation's capital. I had the false impression that things would be different in DC.

Ciria and I lived in relatively new apartments in Washington. DC. Race tensions and animosity were still high after the social protests of the 1950s and 1960s. I would shop alone as Ciria was with Ed frequently. I was unafraid to shop at the underground shopping area near Lafayette Park. I was confused, however, and felt insulted when the checkout clerk was rude and told me I was not liked because I was white. I wanted to explain that I was Hispanic and did not have a racist cell in my body. I knew it was no use, however. Azu, a black Nigerian with a strong accent, had warned me I would not be accepted. When he spoke, it was obvious he was not from DC and was not welcomed even though he was black.

I lived with Ciria that summer and fall. I dined nightly at international restaurants with Azu until I went to New Mexico at Thanksgiving. Needless to say, I gained ten pounds despite my regular tennis playing with Azu. I left for New Mexico in a rush to catch an airplane to New Mexico and did not pay the rent. Ciria and I were evicted immediately. I learned the lesson about no grace in the big city right away. It was my fault, and I felt bad.

After Ciria and I were evicted, I accepted the offer to move in with Bill and Dexanne. Bill was a lawyer I worked with in Congressman Badillo's office. I lived with them until I could move into my efficiency apartment on M Street in the District. An efficiency apartment was basically a one/two-room apartment. Bill helped me move and buy some minimal furniture to furnish my new apartment. Once I moved in alone, I started to ponder life. I lived in a small but nice apartment and was making a good salary on Capitol Hill. This was not a bad life for a poor Hispanic who came from a broken home and was in a foster home. The Housing and Urban Development Building (HUD) was not far from me. Yet I felt uncomfortable every time I looked out my efficiency apartment. I also thought about life's meaning. There were so many contradictions.

Just a few blocks away, I could see burned buildings and homeless people living in partially walled apartments, trying to stay warm in our nation's capital city. I tried to reconcile the dichotomy. Down the street was HUD. In the other direction, but not far, were homeless people. I was told that urban renewal had come through after the anti-war and civil rights riots burned sections of Washington in the 1960s. I was told that the people living in the new apartments created much resentment in the other folks. The well-off yuppies (as we were called) were living next to the poor. It was hard for me to reason why this was happening, and I knew why the crime rate was so high in the District. The poor resented the rich professionals moving into high-rise apartments near them. It was a contrast between the seemingly rich and poor. There was one experience that really shook me.

I jogged by the Potomac River daily when I lived in the efficiency apartment. A concerned black lady warned me one day that a man was killed the week before. I asked the lady why he was murdered. Her response shook me.

"He was killed because he was white and jogging."

I was shocked and discontinued my jogging by the Potomac River.

The episode was enough to scare me away from the cut-throat political world. When I went home to New Mexico, I learned that Harrison Hagan "Jack" Schmitt, a civilian geologist and former astronaut, had defeated long-serving New Mexico U.S. Senator Joseph Montoya with a decisive victory. The U.S. Senator-elect was looking for someone with Capitol Hill and bilingual education experience. I fit the requirements. I was interviewed when I went to New Mexico on Thanksgiving vacation. I was offered a job and took it right away and was surprised.

The offer was unexpected. My only Hill experience was working on the House side for a Democrat from South Bronx, New York. Senator Schmitt ran as a Republican. Was that acceptable? I had worked for a Democrat. I have since learned that political parties were not as hostile to each other back then.

I accepted the offer because I was from New Mexico and wanted to leave the work for Congressman Badillo and the borough of the South Bronx. New York was a different world, and I knew New Mexico well. I was a Hispanic educator and had lived in the north and south of New Mexico. New York City was new to me. I did not know the big city or understand the culture.

Puerto Rico was different from New Mexico. Both places were once under Spanish control, and both places spoke Spanish. However, NYC was urban and sprawling while New Mexico was relatively rural and had isolated large cities, like Albuquerque, that were surrounded by mountains. Puerto Rico and New Mexico were very different, too. Both were Hispanic, but their cultures were very different.

Both New Mexicans and Puerto Ricans, and even Cubans, spoke Spanish. They were, however, different cultures. I found myself at the crossroads of two Hispanic cultures, so I left Congressman Badillo's office. I was eager to work for a U.S. Senator from my home state. I could speak New Mexican Spanish and knew the culture.

The physical geography of the continental U.S. states was different, too. When I first moved to Washington, DC to live with Ciria, I admired the lush, beautiful green trees and grass. I also felt claustrophobic, however, as I could not see the horizon nor the coming rainstorms. I would see them coming from a distance of over fifty miles in Las Cruces and Albu-querque. New Mexico was much different geographically.

Anyway, while I lived on M Street in my efficiency apartment in downtown DC, I remembered what Billy Graham had said at an Albuquer-que crusade I attended at the insistence of a sweet neighbor, Catherine, in 1975. She was a devout Christian, and I considered myself a good Catholic.

I went with her to the crusade. I heard the message that Jesus loves you and is standing at the door knocking. He was just waiting for an invi-tation to come in and take over your life. I gave in to the prompting of my friend and went down the crusade stairs to go to the floor as an invitation was given. I was a little confused because I was Catholic and had been bap-tized and confirmed. I kept all the Holy Days of obligation, went to confes-sion on Saturdays weekly, said the rosary regularly, and fasted during Lent. I knew God and Jesus and kept all the obligations of the Catholic Church. Why did I have to go forward and "receive Christ?" I was Catholic. All the others walking forward were not Catholic, I thought. I did not have to go forward. In my opinion, I was going to Heaven and all the people who had not been Catholic were not. I went forward to please my friend and remembered what the Reverand Graham said: "Just seek Him, and in-vite him in your heart."

When I was pondering life in DC, I remembered Graham's words. I went to work in the Dirksen Senate Office Building and came home nightly to "seek" God. I got out my King James Version of the Bible and started to read in Genesis. I was a good Catholic but had never read the Bible myself. I read my missalettes and other Catholic literature but had never read the Bible. I guess I am living proof of God's grace because I challenged Him to "come into my life" every night for about two weeks after I came home from work.

One night, after my two week quest, a ray of light came into my room in the corner. At first, I thought it was a reflection from outside of my sev-enth-floor efficiency apartment in downtown DC. I stood up and looked outside. There were no lights coming into my efficiency apartment. I went back to my sleeper sofa and stared at the effervescent light.

I finally said, "Oh, that is you, God. You are coming into my life. I get it now. That is how you meet those who are seeking You."

I fell asleep that night knowing that I had had a personal encounter with the living God or God's own messenger.

I awoke the next morning feeling a peace and joy that is still indescribable. I dressed and went to the Senator's office. I was eager to tell others about my experience from the night before. When I passed Nancy's desk on my way to mine, I wanted to shout to her or Carol behind her that I encountered God the night before. I waited and bounced past them with unspeakable joy that day.

When I arrived at my desk, I was eager to tell Linda about my experience the night before. After all, she was bubbly and told me about her EST experience in California as soon as she returned. I did not expect her reaction to my story, however.

Linda looked puzzled after I told her what had happened. She calmly asked me how much I had to drink the night before. When I told her I had been on a quest and that I had not been drinking at all, she asked me what drugs I was taking.

"No drugs," I told her.

I felt deflated. I was surprised and confused that Linda did not believe my story. I stopped talking about my experience to other Senator staffers after no one believed me and looked at me with raised eyebrows. I just went to work and kept my encounter to myself. I had been the same person they had worked alongside for months. I just had a real spiritual experience, and no one believed me. So, I stopped telling my story.

Two events made me ponder life as I worked on the Hill.

A friend from New Mexico came to DC and came "out of the closet" to proclaim he was gay. He and his partner invited me to understand their world and join them as they went to a gay bar on Capitol Hill. I was determined to be open-minded and tolerant, so I accepted his invitation to accompany him and his friends.

Resolute to get into their heads and understand their lifestyle, I asked many questions and just listened as they shared their gay experiences. What I learned from these gay men made a lasting impression on me. It was the foundation for what I believe about homosexuality today.

I learned that many gay people endured sexual trauma or rejection as children. I learned that many had dominating opposite-sex members who did not accept them. I learned about anal cutting to accommodate a partner. I learned about multiple sexual encounters every night. I also learned about "yellow showers" where they showered each other with urine. I left the gay bar with a further understanding. I left feeling very sorry for the people I interviewed. I tried to reconcile this freedom to do sexually brutal things to each other with the "gay" lifestyle. I could not. It was not a religious idea but common sense. They were not happy or gay. They were looking for acceptance from these other people who shared their lifestyle.

What I felt after listening most of the night was pity for them. They were not living a free or gay lifestyle. I was confused that they could not see that freedom to mutilate and give into every urge was not freedom but bondage to their own desire or that of someone else's urge. There was nothing gay or happy about what I learned. My plan and intention that night was to be tolerant and accepting. What I learned was bondage, exploitation, cruelty, and abuse. So many had exchanged freedom for bondage to desires. It was a very sad evening to me and formed my beliefs.

The second event took place when I finally went to work for Senator Harrison Schmitt. Linda left early on Friday and told us she was flying to a conference in California. When she returned a week later, she told me that she had gotten in touch with her inner self and was completely uninhibited now. Linda told me about her nude encounters with several other attendees at the conference. She told me that they ate and slept in the same room. She told me about her defecating and urinating at will and in front of others.

Again, Linda's activity did not seem "freeing" to me. Lack of restraint and giving in to every bodily urge did not seem like freedom or self-actualization to me. It seemed like bondage to infantile urges. We trained toddlers not to do what they did as adults. I was confused as to why Linda felt she had been freed. Her experience has stuck with me. I often think about the other attendees. I feel sorry that they believed a lie about freedom.

12

Baseball on the Hill

I was hired to work as a receptionist for newly elected Senator Harrison "Jack" Schmitt. I would receive, open, and sort mail. I also greeted people who came in or wanted to talk to the Senator or one of his staffers on the telephone. Diana or Nancy saw leadership potential in me. One of these two women nominated me for a leadership role. I was eventually nominated to be the head legislative correspondent.

My responsibilities included screening college interns, hiring them, and supervising them. I really enjoyed working with college students. There were many applicants, and I reviewed everyone carefully. One intern named Tony was on the New Mexico coed delegation team. He was hotheaded and contested many close calls. Tony returned to college in New Mexico after his internship. I was informed that he lost his life in a barfight after his return. It was sad to me. I wish I had spent more time counseling him that his argumentative spirit was not good and would cause much trouble. It finally cost him his life.

Another responsibility I had was to be coach, captain, and pitcher of the Senator's coed high arch softball team that became the New Mexico Delegation Team. I loved the responsibility and took our practices seriously. I had only learned the skill from Mercy and from our pick-up games in the housing projects. (My experience was similar to the movie *The Sandlot*.)

Senator Schmitt played first base on our team when he was there. When he was absent, Congressman Manuel Lujan from the New Mexico delegation played first base. The other U.S. Senator from New Mexico, Senator Pete Domenici, never played with us. Some of his staff did, though.

Congressman Lujan broke his finger after he caught a throw to him from me, the pitcher. It was high-arch softball, but occasionally there was a line drive back at me. I deflected the ball, picked it up, and threw it to first base to get the runner out after he ran. Congressman Lujan caught it awkwardly as he was not expecting the throw. Needless to say, I felt bad. We replaced him at first base and continued to play as he went to the hospital to get a splint.

Senator Schmitt held staff meetings on Fridays. As the legislative correspondent, I had to give a weekly report on constituent mail. I was responsible for drafting a response to the constituents based on their input and having the Senator edit it and return it to me the next week. We purchased an autopen with his signature and after proofing the response, we would send a timely reply to the New Mexican constituents. On occasion, we would write a letter to an important national figure, but mostly Diana, his administrative assistant, handled mail from other national leaders.

Senator Schmitt was a good man. He was responsive and wanted to serve his constituency. He had never served as a politician before. He defeated Senator Montoya because of Montoya's seemingly rude comment about the "monkey from the moon" as Schmitt was an astronaut. Schmitt's popularity stemmed from being the first civilian to fly on an Apollo mission to the moon. He was a geologist astronaut who walked on the moon and brought back the moon rocks. These samples are still on display at the Air and Space Museum as part of the Smithsonian museums in Washington, DC. A display of his mission, Apollo 17, and Senator Harrison Hagan "Jack" Schmitt is there also. He was my boss, and I loved working for him. Frequently, I would ponder how a poor Hispanic girl who was left to die and was in a foster home worked on Capitol Hill, first for a U.S. congressman and then for a U.S. Senator. There was a hand guiding me. I did not know that it was God.

13

The Blind Date

Another responsibility I had as a legislative correspondent for Senator Schmitt was to supervise the employees who worked in the Senate Annex building. The Senate Annex was a converted hotel. Clara, a co-worker from New Mexico, and I would take individual showers after our lunch jog around the Mall area between the Capitol and the Washington Memorial. I loved the break from office work.

I always respected Laura who seemed to juggle work and being a wife and mother. She left work often to take care of motherly duties. It was Laura who suggested the name "Hagan" for our new robo-machine used to write responses to New Mexican constituents. I believed the new technology at the time was cool. Hagan, as the new machine was called, mass-produced an automated response to constituents.

Mike, Tony's childhood friend from Pennsylvania, had married Clara and moved to Washington, DC to work for the FBI. Clara was hired to work for the FBI in DC then went to work for Senator Schmitt as she was from Pojoaque in northern New Mexico. Clara became my fast friend and made me laugh a lot. Mike connected with his childhood friend, and they spent weekends together.

Clara had befriended me and was insistent on setting me up on a blind date with Mike's childhood friend named Tony. I was seeing a Hispanic lawyer at the time and was not interested. I told this to Clara. She was persistent. She said Tony and I went together. We were both minorities. (He was an Arab, and I was Hispanic.) Clara appealed to my compassion and said that Mike's childhood friend from Pottsville, Pennsylvania, was lonely and heartbroken as he had recently broken up with his long-time girlfriend. Mike, on the other hand, was trying to persuade his friend. They were close and grew up together in Pottsville. Mike went to the public school, and his friend graduated from the Catholic school. Mike's friend, Tony, went to Catholic school his entire life and was an altar boy in the Catholic church.

Tony Koury was Mike's friend. Tony moved to DC as a territory representative for Michelin Tire Corporation. He was hired after he graduated from Penn State University and worked in Edison, New Jersey, and Long Island, New York. Tony's girlfriend broke up with him while Tony was in training for Michelin. His mom, Bernadette, felt bad and had been praying that God would send Tony a wife. Tony, a new Christian, trusted God and stopped looking for a wife as he believed God would find one for him.

Both Tony and I finally agreed to meet each other after work on a Friday night. Tony was living near Clara and Mike in Laurel, Maryland. The plan was for Tony to come over to meet me after we got home at about 7:30. I was not crazy about a blind date, so I wore my least favorite dress, and my hair needed to be washed. I agreed because Clara had been so nice and hospitable to me. Meeting Mike's friend was the least I could do.

Tony, too, was reluctant to go on another arranged "blind" date. He had had two bad experiences before. One time a friend had arranged for horseback riding with a blind date. Tony said that the excursion was going well as the blind date was pretty and nice. The horses then turned around a corner. Tony's date turned back to wait for him and show him the way.

Then Tony noticed that his date's one eye stayed looking straight while the other one looked at him. His date had a glass eye! There was nothing wrong with a partially blind girl. He just did not know. He cornered his friend and grilled him on why he did not reveal that his "blind" date was blind in one eye before he asked Tony to join him.

The next time Mike invited Tony to go on a blind date, Tony asked the obvious question: "Is the date blind?" Mike replied that she was not blind or partially blind and invited Tony and his date to a pool party at his apartment complex. Tony and the young woman agreed to meet at the pool.

Everything went well. The date was endowed in the right areas and wore a pretty bikini. She sat next to Tony after he played a fun game of pool volleyball. She gave him a towel to dry before she put her hand on his leg.

Tony complimented his date on her pretty hands as not many women painted their nails at the time. Tony had a good time with this date and thought she could be the one for him. She was pretty and nice. She was built in the right places, and he grew to like her. He was thinking about asking her out on a date—not arranged—when she stood up to walk to the lady's room. She was cold and went to get dressed.

The Blind Date

Then Tony noticed. As she walked back to where he was sitting, Tony saw her silhouette as the light was behind her and her arms were swinging. His date was not blind. Nor did she have a glass eye. But she only had one hand! Tony wanted to evaporate! He could have complimented her on several parts of her body. But no, he chose to compliment her "hands." He had said "hands," but she only had one hand! He wanted to jump in the pool and never come out again.

Needless to say, Tony was leery of blind dates. He asked Mike if I was blind. He asked Mike if I had *both* hands. He finally asked Mike if I had any physical defects he should know about. There was nothing wrong with a nice and pretty girl who had physical challenges, he assured Mike. He just wanted to know beforehand. Tony still felt horrible about complimenting the one-handed date about her "hands" when she only had one hand!

Clara and I rode the Baltimore and Ohio train (B&O) from Union Station by Capitol Hill and arrived at Clara and Mike's home after 7:30 that Friday night. We waited for Tony to arrive as we ate and engaged in small talk. We waited and we waited. Finally, Tony called Mike at about 11:00 p.m. and told Mike that he had taken his phone off the hook so he could take a nap before meeting his new blind date. Mike tried to call several times and received a weird busy signal. Mike apologized several times for his friend.

When Tony finally called, he told Mike he was not going to come over because he was tired, and it was too late to go to Mike's house. Mike was hot and replied, "Get your butt over here!" Tony sensed the seriousness in Mike's voice and drove over to their house right away.

Tony came in and slouched in a chair by the door. He was cute enough and had a muscular build. He was short and looked shorter as he slouched. We obligingly met each other, and I followed Clara into the kitchen. I overheard Tony asking Mike what my name was again. I knew my name was unusual and many people asked me to pronounce it a second time. I thought, however, that Tony was rude. He was late, did not want to keep an agreement, slouched in the chair, and then asked for my name a second time. He was very rude.

I knew that I did not want to "meet" Tony again. My obligation to Clara had been fulfilled. My life would go on. I was happy working on the Hill. I forgot about Tony. I would work, play coed slow-pitch softball with the delegation, and go to frequent lobbyist receptions on the Hill. Then I received a phone call from Clara.

Clara knew I loved to watch professional basketball. She told me she had four tickets to the Capitol Center to watch the Bullets and the Bucks. She asked me if I wanted to go to an NBA game with her and Mike. I said, "Sure." Then she told me the fourth ticket would be offered to Tony. I did not know at the time that Mike had called Tony to tell him I would be his date for the game.

We both agreed to go watch the game, and I rode to the Capitol Center with Mike and Clara. Tony and I sat next to each other and said very little as we watched the game. The first conversation we actually had was about the bridges in our mouths. We each had a bridge over the same teeth on the same side of our mouth. It was just small talk as we watched the game.

When the game was over, I asked the other three if they wanted to join me to go to a party on Capitol Hill. They all agreed to go, and Tony asked me to ride with him in his white Buick Regal. I thought it was clean and pretty. It had burgundy seats. I also thought it was nice that Tony opened the door for me. Maybe he had some gentlemanly qualities after all.

As we rode to the party, I noticed a button lying in Tony's console. It said. "Jesus '76" on it. Surprised, I asked Tony if he believed in Jesus. He said, "Yes. I am a born-again Christian." Still surprised by his answer, I asked Tony if I could share my light experience with him. I told him that I had stopped telling others because no one believed me. He said that I could tell him spiritual experiences. So, I told him about the light that shone into my room after I spent weeks searching for God in a Bible I did not understand. I told Tony about my Billy Graham Crusade attendance.

Tony said calmly that God enters a life when one asks for God to enter. He told me he had attended the Jesus Festival in 1976 and that is why he had the button. I was surprised that he listened to my story. I was surprised that he did not mock nor make fun of me. We went on to the party, and he drove me home. I knew I had found someone I could talk to about my experience. I felt happy that I could talk to Tony about spiritual matters.

14

TAG

Tony called me after a few days. He was not prompted nor encouraged by a friend. He had to find someone who was equally yoked. Tony's family had admonished him not to date nor marry someone who was not a Christian. I was Catholic but had not confessed to follow God alone, even though I faithfully attended Confession on Saturdays while I was in New Mexico. Tony's whole family had decided to follow Jesus alone although his mom attended a Bible study at Nativity Blessed Virgin Mary Catholic School. His mom still sang in the choir at St. Patrick's Catholic Church, too.

I was a good Catholic girl. Every Saturday I confessed to a waiting Catholic priest in a confessional. I started my prayer of repentance with, "Bless me, Father, for I have sinned. It has been a week since my last confession." I then told the priest through the screen all the sins I committed, or thought about committing, throughout the week. The priest (or Father as we called him) would give to me my prayers of penance. I walked to the altar with a rosary as needed and said my prayers of penance. I remember my Catholic friends commenting, "Gee man, you sinned a lot!" as I walked back from the altar where I said my lengthy prayers of repentance.

I never knew they were watching me. I was a good Catholic. I was careful not to think bad thoughts, not to steal, and not to tell a lie until I received the host at Communion the next morning. I could then resume my activities during the week as I knew I would confess to the priest and say my prayers of repentance next Saturday.

Tony's official first date request to this very Catholic lady was to his church. It was held on Tuesday nights at a rented Presbyterian Church on Massachusetts Avenue near the District but in Maryland. He had attended that church after his mom found it for him when he moved to the nation's capital. It was another denominational church on Sundays but was rented to TAG (Take and Give) on Tuesday nights.

A man named Larry Tomczak and his friend CJ Mahaney started this ministry after Tomczak wrote the book *Clap Your Hands.* Both Mahaney and Tomczak had been Catholic. Tomczak wrote the book to tell Catholics there was more to spirituality than the rules we kept. TAG eventually evolved into the Covenant Life Church in Gaithersburg, Maryland. Wikipedia describes their history:

> Covenant Life Church had its roots in a citywide charismatic prayer meeting called Take and Give (TAG) which ran from 1970 to 1979. TAG began as a small Bible study led by Lydia Little, a Washington, DC area resident who had experienced the *Jesus People* revival in California and wanted to see similar renewal brought to local young people. TAG continued to grow in numbers with the Tuesday night meetings moving from the Blair High School auditorium to a larger auditorium space at Christ Church of Washington. Larry Tomczak and C.J. Mahaney became the main teachers with Jim Orbán (eventual son-in-law of Lydia Little) leading worship and a number of young people taking on other leadership responsibilities as the group grew. At its largest point TAG attracted over 2,000 people, primarily young attendees under the age of 25.
>
> In 1977 a small group of people (55 at the first meeting, many of whom were TAG attendees) began to gather in the basement of a suburban Maryland home. Simultaneously, the TAG ministry began to wind down and met for the last time in December 1979.[5]

I was reluctant to attend a church service that was on a Tuesday night, but I went with Tony because I was on a spiritual quest, and I wanted to know more. We entered TAG, and I was overwhelmed by the number of people who attended church on Tuesdays. I was impressed by the section that signed the message to the deaf. There seemed to be over 300 people in that one section alone. To me, thousands of people were at the service.

We walked in and sat down. Instantly, I observed that this was not a Catholic service. There was no genuflecting or the sign of the cross. They were speaking to the Almighty and Holy God out loud! I wanted to run out of this crazy, cult-like place when I saw people running up to the altar to be healed!

Always one to speak my mind, I told Tony at church that he was a member of a cult! I told Tony that I never wanted to see him again and that I would most certainly not attend his "church service" ever again. I told him, "Goodbye," when the service ended. We rode home in silence.

Ashamed at what I experienced the night before, I told no one about the TAG experience. I disciplined my mind to only focus on work and the softball practice we held after work. We would change at work and travel to the practice field either at Anacostia or the fields near the National Mall.

Tony called me a few days later. I hung up on him. He called back, however, and wanted to talk about my experience. Our "discussion" was mostly me telling him that his church was a crazy place. I told him I would talk to him but would not attend church with him again. So, he just listened as I fumed.

He called me often during that time. He seemed like a nice person. It was hard for me to understand how Mike or Clara tolerated Tony's religious views. Hadn't Mike grown up with Tony? Didn't he know Tony's family? How could Mike and Clara set me up with a member of a religious cult? None of these answers made sense to me. Maybe Tony was not crazy.

When Tony called again weeks later, I accepted his invitation to attend another church service with him., I accepted partially because I could not be a quitter. I would find out for sure if TAG was a cult. We went back to Tony's church service and walked up the stairs past the crowds of people. I could see and hear Larry Tomczak clearly.

His message rang true to me. *Was I a sinner in need of salvation? Did I need to surrender my life to the Lord? Would God direct my path if I just asked Him into my life and let him? That is what Billy Graham had said!*

Running down the stairs, I knew the message was for me, and I had to speak to one of the guys at the altar. I remember crying … sobbing … as I ran down the stairs to the altar. I knew I had to voluntarily surrender my will to God's will and His purpose for my life. He had directed my path after my Billy Graham experience. He came into my room as a shining light. He brought Tony into my life—a Pennsylvania man and a New Mexican woman. Now God was calling me to surrender my strong will to His will. I sobbed as I knew I had to do it. There was *no* coincidence that He directed me out of New Mexico to work on Capitol Hill and ultimately meet Tony and go to his church. I knew that it was *no* coincidence, and I would surrender my life to God. I would let Jesus take control of my life. I surrendered my life to God and let Him take control.

I attended church with Tony every Tuesday for the next 18 months. I learned about the miracles Jesus performed. The stories in the Bible made sense to me now. Jesus, the Son of Almighty God, put on a body suit and came to earth as a man. He was commissioned to be completely man, and yet He had a spiritual identity. He showed mankind that He could heal the sick, forgive the repentant sinner, and rise from the dead. I was reminded that Jesus had the power to forgive all of my sins when I ran down to the altar repeatedly after hearing an altar call. I was told that one complete confession was enough. I was told that the Holy Spirit would bring my sins to mind and that all I needed to do was acknowledge and confess my sins.

But, I argued, Jesus did not *know* all of my sins because I had not confessed them. I was a faithful Catholic who went to confession every Saturday to confess my sins. I was told I did not need to do that anymore. Once I accepted Christ into my life, all my sins were forgiven. I was born again. I had a new life! I was told that is the message of the Gospel. It made sense to me. He was punished and died so I would not have to be punished and be separated from God for all the things I did. So, I could live in eternity with God. I got it. I understood it. It was a spiritual truth! It was neither physical nor cognitive. It was a spiritual truth. How could I resist this truth?

Jesus, as God's only Son, had chosen to die for me. He chose to take my punishment. When He left the earth in the Ascension after his resurrection from the dead. He left the Holy Spirit to convict and guide me. It all made sense now. Man had attempted to use and organize the Church for his own purposes. I knew I was not part of an organization of men and women. I knew that I had a personal relationship with God through Christ and now His Holy Spirit. It made sense to me now. I would live by God's rules, not manmade rules. I could not stop reading the Holy Spirit-inspired Word of God. I would be a new person, as Jesus told Nicodemus. I would be born again, not of flesh but of Spirit. I understood it all. My blinders were gone!

Jesus had the power of life and death. He even raised a dead man from his grave. I learned much from TAG, reading the Bible, and from Tony's family. We took trips to Pottsville often after my surrender to Christ. It was important to Tony that I meet his family. We spoke the same spiritual language, and I talked to Tony's mom until two and three a.m. I was hungry for truth, and Tony's mom was happy to share what she learned with me.

I met Tony's older sisters, Antoinette, Susan, and Bernadette. I also met little Georgie, Tony's long-awaited little brother. He did not look like Tony as he was a miracle child born to Tony's stepdad, Jidu, after his biological dad, Tony, died of cancer. I grew to love Jidu and Georgie as I got to know these relatively shy men on my frequent visits to Pottsville.

Tony's biological father, Tony or "Fatz" as they called him, had been a butcher, store owner, and an artist. Tony painted many religious artworks in and around Pottsville. He painted or restored all the statues in the Catholic churches in

Tony's dad painted DaVinci's Last Supper. This canvas hangs in our dining room.

Schuylkill County. The name "Koury" (or "Khouri" as it is often spelled) literally means "son of the priest." Tony's ancestors in Lebanon and Syria were Maronite Catholics. They were allowed to marry. Tony's great-grand-

John (Jidu) and his best friend, Tony

father, Joseph, was a Maronite priest. Tony's father was a good Catholic. He gave much to the Catholic Church with the artistic gifts he was given. We still have a large oil painting of the Last Supper hanging in our dining room. Tony's dad painted a replica of the masterpiece by Leonardo DaVinci. Tony's dad also painted the outfield fence advertisements at Railway Park where the Little League Baseball players played in Pottsville. He was a gifted artist.

Jidu (Tony's stepdad—Jidu is Arabic for grandfather) was Tony Sr.'s best friend and volunteered for Tony Sr. at the Koury Blue Front Market in Pottsville. Jidu gave up his job as a machinist and never married. He then took a job walking the beat as a policeman in downtown Pottsville to check on his mom who was blind and only spoke Arabic. John G. Barket, Jidu, was a good man. He was patient and kind. He spoke little but could be found chopping food in the kitchen. One hilarious story tells it all.

Jidu was not feeling well. His brother, Tom, was visiting and volunteered to take Jidu to the emergency room at the local hospital. Jidu endured several tests and returned to his home hours later. When the two men returned from the hospital, they came into Tony's house and sat down. Tony's mom, who we call Imee, nervously awaited their return. She asked, after a long silence, "Well, what did they find at the hospital?"

Tony (left) and
his half-brother, George

Tom looked puzzled and said, "I don't know." He looked at Imee's curious face and continued. "John didn't say anything, and I did not ask." They were men with few words but good men, nonetheless. I think of a Bible verse when thinking about Jidu. Proverbs 17:27 says, "The one who has knowledge uses words with restraint..." (NIV). Jidu was a man of peace and understanding as he served Pottsville as a policeman.

Jidu's mom and Tony Sr. died about three years apart. Jidu believed it was his responsibility to take care of his best friend's wife and children. He married Bernadette and raised four children. The four children called Jidu "Uncle John" when he came to their house with Tony Sr. When Jidu was going to marry Bernadette, friends asked who she would marry. Tony Jr. replied, "My mom is going to marry my uncle." His friends looked puzzled.

Bernadette and John were blessed with a son when Bernadette was 44 years old. Tony had prayed for a brother for many years. George was 15 years younger than Tony. George looked very Arabic like his dad, and Tony, his older brother, was fair complected and had blue eyes like his dad. They loved each other and never argued. George was shy and soft-spoken like his dad, and Tony was outspoken and outgoing like his dad.

Susan, Tony's older sister, taught me a lot about the spiritual world. She was, as Tony's mom called her, a "wild one." Sue was fascinating to me as I was hungry for spiritual truth. Sue had seen the effects of the hippie and drug culture. She once ran away to live in a commune. She was known for her great artistic ability and looked like her dad and Tony. Sue was once "in tune" with evil spirits, too. Some say she was clairvoyant. Sue told me about her unreformed life, and I was fascinated by all she said during our nightlong chats. She had seen both sides of the spiritual world.

Sue's experiences with the dark side of the spiritual world reminded me of an awakening I had when I watched *The Exorcist* with the bile-vomiting of Linda Blair that helped to lead me to a spiritual awakening. I read the marquee outside the theater in Washington, DC while I waited in the long line to enter the movie theater. I read the newspaper article about the actual exorcism that took place in New Jersey. I watched the whole movie intensely. At the end of it, I was pensive. I thought to myself, *If an evil spirit can possess a person, I want the good spirit to possess me.* It was logical, reasonable, and practical. It was not a religious decision.

Sue recounted her "wild" days during our long chats. She told me about the demons that were her "friends." She described them to me and even drew some of them for me to see. The strange coincidence was when we moved to South Carolina years later, I took our three sons to the old Simpsonville library. Our three sons were encouraged to find books in the children's section. I sat in the little lobby and noticed a book on the shelf. It was titled *Book of Demonology*. I was curious so I went over and brought it back to my seat. There were drawings of demons in the book. They looked like the ones Sue drew for me. I knew she did not write a book and reasoned that the knowledge of demons must be widespread. Again, I reasoned that we live in a spiritual world with agents of good and evil around us. It was a rational, logical insight. It was not religious.

15

"Rocky Roads"

The relationship with Tony had started rocky, but it blossomed the next year as we dated. We attended his church on Tuesdays, and Tony joined Schmitt's Astro-Mitts as a substitute third baseman. My nickname was given to me during this time. Tony would call me in the spring and summer and ask me out for a date. I would frequently respond, "Okay, if you meet me on the baseball field first."

He replied often "Baseball, baseball. That is all you think about!" Tony gave me a nickname during this time. My nickname is Baseball. I still use it in various forms in my communication to Tony. He substituted as my third baseman frequently. We have great memories of that time.

One time, we were supposed to meet on a field in Anacostia to warm up for the game. I called Tony on an old desk phone that I borrowed. I was in a panic and told him that one of our team members had not shown up, and we were going to have to forfeit the game. Tony said he would come right away. Well, our team member parked near the field right after I hung up. Tony was on his way already. That was a good thing considering what happened next.

Our team member rushed to the field. She screamed at the team in a panic, "I left my keys in my car!" I calmly told her we would get them after our inning as the umpire was going to call a forfeit if all our team members were not on the field. She said persistently, "You don't understand! My car is locked!"

I said, "Good, go to third base now."

She insisted, "But my car is still running!" We walked over to her car after the umpire counted us as all there.

What we saw shocked us. Our teammate had left her keys in a running car, and she left a lit cigarette in the ashtray. The cigarette had fallen, and there was a fire blazing in a running locked car! We stopped the game to break the window, unlock the car, turn it off, and put out the fire. Tony arrived during the commotion and was willing to step in and play third base while our teammate calmed down and dealt with the car situation. We won the game but will remember it not for the excellent plays but for a burning car.

We learned much about each other as we dated. The event that formed my opinion about life and human nature was a canoe trip Tony (my future husband) and I took.

We saw a brochure on the way back from Pennsylvania. We decided to spontaneously take a 24-hour ride down the Shenandoah River in Virginia. Neither of us had gone canoeing, but we were going anyway. When we arrived at the launch site, some guys near us asked us what we would do when we capsized and lost our supplies. Tony and I replied that we had no intention of capsizing. The men just laughed and continued to rope their supplies. We put ours in plastic bags just in case.

We boarded our canoe, and I sat in the back so Tony could steer. We spun around as we set off. We spun around again. Then we spun around again and again. Our launch site was still in sight, and we had set off on our voyage over an hour before. Finally, Tony said, "Paddle on the same side." Okay then, I would paddle on the same side as Tony. We spun around again. Then we spun around again and again. We still had twenty-six miles to go, and we had not left the launch site.

Tony turned around in anger and said, "Will you please paddle on the same side?"

Okay, I thought. *As soon as he starts to move, I will paddle on the same side as him.* Maybe it was speed that he wanted after all. We were still near the launch site after two hours. We were both frustrated at the lack of progress.

Tony turned around and exclaimed, "You, get to the front of the canoe so I can keep an eye on you." It was not until that night when he asked me why I would not stay on the same side with my oar.

"Oh," I replied, "I thought you wanted me to row on the same side as you were rowing!" We laughed hard and later found out that the heaviest person should be in the back of the canoe. We think now that it was the transfer of positions that allowed us to row successfully. We learned that clear communication was the center of our confusion and problems. Clear communication is at the center of marriage and society in general. Clear communication involves both the speaker and the hearer. It is important that the hearer "hears" and understands what the speaker actually "says." We rowed successfully for the rest of the journey.

There were other adventures that we had that night, though. We made camp in our little pup tent near a cow pasture that was sectioned off with barbed wire. After we made a nice steak dinner on our newly purchased hibachi grill, we decided to rest for the night in our pup tent. After all, we were going to have to travel 26 miles downstream, and we had only traveled six miles. We had many miles to canoe the next day, so we decided to rest. Well, I did.

Tony reasoned that the cows he heard across the river had dumped their waste near our tent site but did not go across the barbed wire fence behind our campsite. He reasoned that they waded across the river, dropped their stuff, and waded back across the river. Every time I awoke, I stared at the rump on Tony's pants. He did not want the cows to come across the river and walk on us. So, he waited and watched on all fours out of the zippered door all night. I slept well but awoke occasionally to stare at Tony's behind. I just figured he was keeping watch and went back to sleep. It was a good thing, however, that he did not venture out that night.

When we awoke at daybreak, we ventured outside. We saw snake tracks all around our small tent. They were not present when we set up camp but had circled our tent during the night. We were so thankful that neither of us went out that night. We do not know the species, but the snake tracks were big.

We ventured down the river after we packed up for the day. We maneuvered the rapids and never capsized. Our launch friends had laughed at us as we started out together, but we ended up passing them on the river as they were frantically trying to save their beer cans that were floating on the river.

Another adventure on our canoe trip was when I told Tony I was going to take a swim because I was hot. I announced that I would dive off the side because I was comfortable swimming in rivers. Tony looked like the *Incredible Hulk* and had developed his muscles during his rowing (while I frequently put on sunscreen). He looked puzzled and screamed at me, "Do not jump! You will have to board the canoe, and it may capsize! Do not jump!" I did not jump after all.

We were picked up after a successful canoe trip. Whenever we have arguments because of miscommunication, we say, "Row on the same side."

Overconfidence and lack of knowledge both have negative conse-
quences we learned on that trip. We also know that miscommunication is
the source of many conflicts. Our relationship went forward.

On Easter weekend in 1978, Tony invited me to visit his family for the
holiday weekend. I always missed the holidays as a former teacher. I
missed the cards and gifts I would receive from students. Tony knew that
and asked me to join him in Pottsville for Easter.

On Easter morning, he asked for me to come down to receive something. I just knew it was an Easter basket or maybe an Easter bunny that he
or his mom bought from Moots Candy. I went hurriedly downstairs. I
passed Jidu in the kitchen who looked very concerned. I did not know
about the previous conversation Tony had with his stepdad.

Tony had bought an engagement ring and was planning to propose to
me. We had played "What-if" games, but he had not asked me to marry
him. Jidu discussed this with Tony beforehand. "What if she says, 'No'
when you propose?" Tony assured Jidu that he would simply return the
ring if I declined his hand to marry him after he asked.

I rushed down to the dining area and found Tony holding a white
chocolate Easter egg. I exclaimed that I loved white chocolate! Tony per-
sisted, "Look inside." I opened the white chocolate egg, and Tony dropped
to one knee and asked, "Will you marry me?"

Frankly, I was in shock. I had not expected the proposal at this time
even though we joked around about marriage. I was numb and silent. Jidu
listened intently from the other room. It took several promptings by Tony,
but I ultimately said, "Yes. Yes, I will marry you!"

We celebrated Easter and our engagement that day. I was eager to tell
the Senator's staff the next week. Nancy, Carole, Clara, and Laura all had
tears in their eyes when I told them. I think secretly some were living vi-
cariously through my courtship with Tony. Tony was a handsome man. He
was seen by Senate staffers as "a good catch." He would come into the office wearing a suit after work. He was in a contest with his boss, Brent,
about who could lose the most weight. Tony was fit and lean. He would
substitute on our baseball team with his cut-off jeans. He earned the nickname "Thunder Thighs."

We had a wedding to plan. Tony was concerned about my divorce
status and was willing to give up the woman he loved to follow God's Law.
We went to premarital counseling with Pastor Wing in Pottsville. He directed us to the Bible passages about divorce. Tony and I were willing to

give up each other to follow God. We decided it was God's Law to be reconciled with David (1 Cor. 7:11). We had decided that pleasing God was first and foremost. We decided to give up each other to follow Jesus.

When I told David that I decided to follow God's ways and not mine, he said, unconvincingly, that he would follow Jesus so we would be evenly yoked. I then tried, unsuccessfully, to get in touch with David as I made plans to return to New Mexico and remarry him. I was told his family had moved. No one knew their whereabouts.

This was unusual because I spoke to David a few days earlier. We took it as a sign that God was blocking my return. It was like the Abraham and Isaac story. God wanted to see if we were faithful to obey Him. We were. God provided His own sacrificial lamb.

16

Marriage

Tony and I moved forward with our wedding plans. I had to decide who would walk me up the aisle. My dad had already done it once, but I still resented him and his new family. God was working on my heart. God was working on my heart to forgive him, but it was hard. We both knew I was his "I baby."

My decision to leave Albuquerque to take a job on Capitol Hill was partially based on my feelings of resentment. I knew I needed a fresh start. Daddy followed me and lived in Virginia. I believed that he moved there to try to repair our relationship after I left New Mexico. He moved his new family to a small town in Virginia.

Tony visited my dad and my dad's family with me. He would often remark that my dad was a real Archie Bunker, a TV personality from a sit-com in the 1970s. Bunker was very opinionated. I did not argue with Tony. My dad told Tony and me historical and autobiographical stories about his life in Virginia, his stepdad, and his sister. He took us to visit the Massa-nutten Military Academy and talked to us about the young men who fought from there. I get my love of history and of books from Daddy.

When Tony and I planned our wedding, Daddy said he had heart problems. He said he was not going to be able to attend the small wedding. Who else could I ask to give me away? I thought about Senator Harrison Schmitt. He did not have a daughter of his own. He was not married at the time. He knew Tony and conversed with him when Tony came to the office. Tony was even invited to listen to the Senator's lectures about his adven-tures as a civilian geologist on the Apollo 17 mission to the moon. I asked the Senator and he said, "Yes. I would be honored to walk you up the aisle."

Years later, when I ran for South Carolina State House District 27, Tony was asked why he did not tell anyone he was an astronaut. The local paper ran an article about me and asked the trivia question, "Which candidate was escorted *down* the aisle?" Senator Schmitt escorted me *up* the aisle. Tony just laughed at the question. He escorted me *down* the aisle after we were wed as man and wife.

Our wedding was small. Only Tony's family, our closest friends, and the Senator's staff were invited. We were on the East Coast, and I was going to introduce Tony to my family when we went to New Mexico. Our evening ceremony overlooked the lush green field in Maryland. We planned to rehearse that morning and then have lunch. My sisters did not attend my wedding to Tony. We had a disagreement because I left the Catholic Church. Linda told me that our Catholic faith prepared me. She had a point. We were planning a trip to New Mexico so "la familia" could get to know my Arab husband from Pennsylvania.

Mr. Smith was the first one to greet us that day. Mr. Smith was a photographer from Pottsville. Tony worked for Mr. Smith when he was young. I still think it is Mr. Smith who is most responsible for Tony knowing how to fix anything. Mr. Smith would instruct Tony to paint or rewire something. He would not give Tony instructions but would let Tony figure it out on his own. I think it was dangerous to let a teenager rewire something on his own, but Mr. Smith did, and Tony was usually successful. Mr. Smith gave us our huge wedding album with all the professional photographs he took as a wedding gift. I treasure it and keep it close to me.

U.S. Senator Harrison Hagan "Jack" Schmitt escorting me at our wedding

We danced the Wedding Marcha at our wedding with Ciria and Ed leading the march. As mentioned, the wedding reception was small and at our apartment clubhouse in Maryland. I did not invite all the college interns that I supervised in the Senator's office. When Bea caught the bouquet, another young man caught the garter. No one knew who he was! The tradition was to have the one who caught the garter place it on the leg of the one who caught the flowers.

It turns out that this unknown young man, featured in our wedding album in several places, was the brother of one of the college interns I supervised. He assumed that the interns were invited and, since his brother couldn't make it, he could come to our wedding in his brother's place. We still do not know his name, but he is featured in our wedding album.

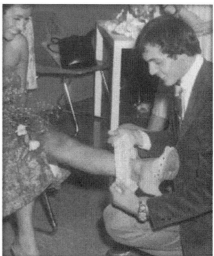

The Wedding Marcha and unknown garter catcher

Before we got married, Tony received a promotion to the training department of Michelin Tire Corporation. It was based out of New York, and Tony would spend three weeks in New York and three weeks in the field to train the new rep. We decided that I would not move to New York with him but would stay in our new apartment and see him when he came home. We knew that the training department was a temporary assignment and that he would be promoted within a year.

Tony and I had decided to let God direct our paths as we committed our marriage to him.

Farewell party for me in U.S. Senator Schmitt's office

17

California

We had decided to buy a townhouse in Gaithersburg, Mary-land, before we got married to build equity instead of renting. We would take a two-week honeymoon and move into our newly purchased townhouse on Barn Swallow Terrace when we returned. We got cold feet about getting into debt with a mortgage payment. We did not know what to do. God knew the future. He would direct our path. Tony and I decided to kneel down and pray over a letter of cancellation to the realtor as we had recently paid a downpayment to start building our town-home. We then put the letter of cancellation in the mail and went on our honeymoon.

We went on a glorious honeymoon to Hilton Head, South Carolina, Underground Atlanta, Georgia, and Disney World in Florida. We returned to our apartment, and there was a knock at the door shortly afterward. It was our neighbor. The letter we prayed over was in her hand. She said it was returned to her apartment.

We looked at the letter puzzled. It was stamped "Return to sender, address unknown." Tony whipped out the realtor's card to compare the address. It was identical. We looked at each other and remembered our prayer. God was directing us. We were supposed to buy the townhouse. Our cancellation was returned to us. We moved in, and he left for New York. I stayed working for the Senator and lived in our townhouse for only three months.

Tony received a promotion in January just six months after he was assigned to the training department. He was offered the position of assis-tant district manager. He was the youngest person at Michelin to be offered this position. It was for the Los Angeles, California district. The territory covered L.A. County south to the Mexican border. The territory also covered the east to Las Vegas. When he told me about the offer, I was sad. I loved working for the Senator and did not want to move to California.

One of the questions Tony always asked me was, "Will you give up your career to raise our kids?"

My answer was always the same. "Yes, I will give up my career to raise our kids." We were about to be tested again.

I finally agreed and applied for a congressional job working in California. It was not as glorious as working on Capitol Hill, but I knew the political system and knew I could help the district office. I accepted the offer to work and made to leave the job I loved.

The morning that the Senator's office planned a farewell party for me, I decided to take an early pregnancy test. I was surprised and elated when I saw the circle in the urine sample. I was expecting our first child, and I knew I would not work but would stay home to raise our child. I had told Tony as much, and I meant it. We were able to tell the Senator's staff at the party.

We would need to sell our townhouse and find a place to live in Tony's district. Our townhouse in Maryland still had unpacked boxes as we had only owned it for three months. The movers thought someone else had been called to pack for us. The truth was that we had never unpacked the boxes. Tony was in New York, and I rode the Amtrack or Baltimore and Ohio (B&O) to DC and returned home to eat and sleep. There was little time to unpack boxes as I rested on the weekends.

We bought our lot to build a townhouse in Maryland for $48,000. We sold it six months later for $60,000. We made enough money to place a down payment on a condominium in California. God knew the future and blocked our cancellation letter. We would have never had the money to place a downpayment in Mission Viejo, California, if we had not bought the townhouse in Maryland.

God was directing our path as we trusted our future to Him. We flew to California by way of Las Vegas. I was too nauseous to appreciate the sites. I was still nauseous and very tired when we arrived at our hotel across from Disneyland. I jokingly called it the "Penny Pincher Inn," but it was advertised by the name Penny Saver Inn.

We ate a big breakfast daily, and Tony went to work. I went back to the room and slept. My only friend while we lived there, waiting for our condominium to be vacated, was a Hispanic maid. She took care of me after

I told her I had morning sickness and was carrying my first child. She was nice and brought me tea to drink daily.

I could not help but wonder if she was legal or illegal. We only spoke Spanish to each other, and I frequently remembered my work on the issue of illegal immigration on the Hill. The Senator gave each staffer an issue to research and write about. It was to be our specialty, and we would report our findings to him on occasion. Mine was the issue of illegal immigration.

The professor at MIT (Massachusetts Institute of Technology) did the research for me as a Senate staffer. I quoted him often when I sat near the Senator as he testified (being a border-state U.S. Senator) before the Senate Judiciary Committee on the Immigration Bill S.2252.

This issue was near to my heart because I was born in Las Cruces, less than 40 miles from the frontera (border). The cause of border problems and the solution to those problems is rooted in economics and ideology. I thought about my research and how this maid just wanted to work to send money to her family in South America. Senator Schmitt testified (after editing my draft) that there were "push" and "pull" factors. The push was poverty and politics.

The pull factors included the U.S.' desire for cheap labor. Now these poor people are caught in an ideological war. They are being exploited for ideology and used by drug dealers. Most poor migrants want to work and provide a better life for their families. They are welcomed or are turned away for politics. U.S. laws should be enforced, but the reasons they risk the long voyage should be addressed. Why don't healthy corporations get their workforce from Central and South America instead of Asia? Corporations can have cheap labor and protect their interests. It can be a win-win-win situation for all interested parties. Instead, migrants are exploited for money and political ideology.

Finding a church to worship and serve was important to us. We found a church in Mission Viejo called Grace Community Church. Tony was persuaded to teach second grade Sunday School while I was pregnant.

We met some dear friends, Liz and John, at church. They had a little baby boy named John. I fell in love with him and held him every chance I got. I asked the Lord to give me a baby just like him. Coincidentally, our firstborn son would be born on John's first birthday. Our son's middle name would be "John."

My pregnancy in California was relatively easy although our son was born three weeks early. It was a blessing that he was for I had gained almost sixty pounds at his birth.

There were several incidents as I drove our little MGB in my rather enlarged state. In one such incident, I pinned a gas station attendant. We lived in California in the middle of the Jimmy Carter presidency. There were long gas lines to wait in during the summer of 1979. I had waited almost an hour in a line to fill up my MGB. I was hot and tired and wanted to get home to rest after a long day.

All the commotion started as I was in this state. I was large, hot, and very pregnant. The gas station attendant motioned for me to drive back to the other pump. I thought, *I just did that!* He was yelling at this point and motioning hysterically at me. I thought, *What does this guy want from me? Can't he tell that I am very pregnant, hot, tired, and in a small car?* I indignantly got out of the MGB to see that I had just pinned a gas attendant behind my car! The car behind me could not move right away because of the long line and the bumper-to-bumper cars behind him.

I felt so bad for the guy and quickly got in my car to move up and release him. He hobbled back inside the gas station with the help of his friends. He gave me a sour look as I drove off after I filled my tank. This unfortunate incident was forgotten when I held our firstborn son.

18

Focal Point

The original due date was October 7 for our first son. My amniotic fluid sack broke early in the morning on September 13. Tony and I were determined to have a natural childbirth. We had taken Lamaze classes to learn about his role and my controlled breathing during labor. When my water broke, we grabbed my focal point. It was the Jesus button that was on his console on our first date. It was the center of our first serious conversation, so I chose it to use during labor. When I arrived at the hospital, I was two centimeters dilated and one centimeter effaced. The OB-GYN instructed the nurse to give me Pitocin to speed up labor since my water had broken already. She obeyed orders.

I did my Lamaze breathing throughout the day thinking this was how it was done. At 11:00, the doctor called to see how I was progressing. When he learned it was slow, he told the nurse to increase the Pitocin. She did and repeated the same thing at 1:30. When the new shift labor and delivery nurse came on duty at 3:30, she said something was wrong. If I had been given the amount of Pitocin prescribed over the period of time I was there, I (in her words) should have flown to the moon.

The nurse examined the dispenser only to find it defective. The Pitocin was not going in like prescribed. It was dripping on the floor. The nurse called the doctor and relayed the situation. He told her to give me the same amount as the last one prescribed. She did, and I immediately went into hard labor. She examined me and said the baby had crowned and for me not to push because I would tear. She called for the ER doctor. He was busy attending to another patient. She asked if there was another OBGYN available. There were none.

She threw the head and foot covering to Tony and wheeled me into the delivery room. I begged her to deliver my baby as I could not stop the pushing anymore.

She replied, "I will have to wait to see if a doctor arrives."

Tony came flying in about this time. I laughed at his appearance. He had a boat-shaped hat on and another in his hand. He later explained that the nurse gave him a bag of covers, but he was so afraid to miss the birth, he forgot to ask how to put them on. He said he did not know where they had taken me in such a hurry. When he came out of the bathroom, I was gone. He ran down the hall to look for me. He was thrown out of one delivery room when the doctor screamed.

"We already have a dad in here!" the delivery doctor yelled.

Tony then noticed the pregnant woman was still wearing earrings, and I had taken off mine. He had appeared in the wrong room, and he panicked that he would miss the birth.

When Tony finally arrived, just before the doctor, I felt that I needed to blow on his face to prevent hyperventilation instead of vice versa. (Tony was supposed to blow on my face to prevent hyperventilation or premature pushing). The OBGYN arrived just in time to give me an episiotomy before I tore. He yanked off his tie and said, "Push." I did, and our son came out with such force that blood splattered on the doctor and the back wall. The trauma was all worth it when I held and nursed our firstborn son, Anthony John Koury III, named after his dad and grandfather.

TJ (short for Tony Jr.) and I did everything together. Tony traveled much, and I drove TJ in the MGB everywhere. Liz and John noticed how talkative was TJ. I think that was because I talked to him all the time and never left TJ with a babysitter. He was my constant companion.

One day, Tony came home, and I announced that TJ and I wanted to show something to him. We walked to the pool in our development, and I put TJ on the edge of the pool, then jumped in and went to the other side. I counted one, two, three, and TJ, in his diaper, plopped in the water and doggy-paddled to me. He never came up for a breath. He was only eight months old.

He was a precocious baby who took swimming lessons. We didn't live far from the Olympic training pool in Mission Viejo. Mothers were considered inept if they did not teach their babies how to swim at a very early age. So, I enrolled TJ in mommy and me swim classes when he was only six months old. Eventually, he would be on a swim team for ten years and teach scuba lessons at the United States Air Force Academy. I often wonder if this early exposure to the water made him very comfortable in it.

We kept our word and traveled to Taos, New Mexico, to visit some of "la familia." Tony was unprepared for the culture shock when he encountered "la familia." My sister, Linda, and her family were living in a small trailer while they awaited their house to be built. Tony was told to turn by the "house with the pink roof."

"But," Tony exclaimed, "it is dark! Your sister must give us more directions." Turning by the house with the pink roof seemed perfectly good directions to us. My sister then gave more directions to Tony, and we arrived that night.

Tony was not prepared for the accommodation, either. Linda and her husband and four children lived in a small trailer. We slept in a small room where our feet and heads both touched the walls. We are not tall people either. I thought it was very nice that the four children gave up their room for us. Tony lived through our cramped accommodations. He was used to creature comforts.

19

Twins

The fatigue came on suddenly. I was still nursing my oldest son. He never had a bottle nor a pacifier. I served as both. We lived in California. It was unheard of to give your baby a bottle. It was not unusual to hear other mothers say that their child would come home for a swig after preschool.

When I went to the doctor to identify the cause of my great fatigue, he asked, "Could you be pregnant?" I replied that I had not menstruated since I got pregnant with my first. I told the doctor I was still nursing. I told him that I had no clue if I was pregnant and, therefore, did not have a clue about the due date. He took tests to identify the cause of my fatigue.

The pregnancy tests came back positive. I was pregnant. I was in shock. The doctor then sent me to an ultrasound technician to determine the size of the baby and possibly get a due date. I made an appointment and went. Since we did not leave our son with a sitter, I took my son with me. I took him everywhere with me.

The ultrasound technician said she would have to get her boss to confirm what she was seeing on the screen. They both came back to my room. He studied the ultrasound images and quietly discussed his findings with the ultrasound technician. I was getting concerned that something was wrong as I waited for their discussion to end. They both eventually turned to me and said, "Congratulations! We have never identified two sacs this early in a pregnancy. You are carrying twins, Mrs. Koury!"

My first feeling was that of surprise. I did not know I was pregnant until that day and certainly did not suspect I was carrying twins! I should have suspected it as there were twins on both sides of our family. My maternal grandma was a twin, but her twin sister died at birth. Tony's

iBaby

grandfather was one of 21 children. There were three sets of twins in his grandfather's family. We should have expected it but did not.

Michelin gave expectant employees $50 dollars per child. My first thought was that Tony would be happy to receive $100 from Michelin. My second thought was how was I going to tell Tony the news that we were going to have twins. Then I thought of the perfect plan.

I would say to Tony, "Greasing the pig, here boss," when I was applying oil to prevent stretch marks on my abdomen during my first pregnancy. "Greasing the pig, here boss," was a take-off of the scene from the movie *Cool Hand Luke* when Paul Newman had to shake the bush to signify that he was still going to the bathroom while working in a field. My plan was to tell Tony by presenting two porcelain pigs and saying that Michelin was going to give us $100. My plan worked. I presented Tony with the two pigs and a note when he got home. As expected, he was shocked and joyous!

Our thoughts then turned to practical matters. I told Tony that it looked like I was 10 weeks pregnant. We did the calculation. If they were delivered on time, we would have three babies under two. The twins were due on June 7, 1981. We were going to have twins, and I was still nursing my son full time. No wonder I was fatigued. I was feeding four people from one body! Tony commented that he wanted a playmate for TJ. God gave us a playmate for the playmate.

The OBGYN told me that I should wean my oldest son. He had received all the benefits of nursing, and I needed to feed myself and the twins inside of me. So, at three months pregnant with twins, I weaned my oldest. I do not know what the hormonal changes were, but I got very nauseous when I weaned TJ. I threw up often and considered taking Bendectin. I had read about birth defects associated with the nausea drug, so I decided against it. Like she always did when we were younger, my sister, Linda, gave me some practical advice.

Linda said that she, too, was nauseous when she was pregnant. She said she would throw up then go back and fill up. *Yuck*, I thought. I did not feel like eating. Linda told me it was for the benefit of the babies I was carrying. I ate protein bars to supplement my food during this period. I did not want to eat either but ate anyway for the benefit of the babies. Women friends have told me that I could have nursed my oldest son through the twin pregnancy. Maybe I should have continued. The nausea stopped being an issue around five months into my pregnancy. I was scheduled for another ultrasound to find out if everything was progressing well. It was, and the twins were the same size at five months of gestation.

20

The Challenge

I met a new friend, April, at the neighborhood park. She was playing with her son, Nicholas. We struck up a conversation and became fast friends. I told April about my conversion experience, and she was sincerely interested. Before long, she and her husband Bill received the Lord as their Savior and attended church with us. She was a California girl and became a good friend.

When the baby shower I threw for April's second child was over, I went home and rested on the sofa. I did not feel well. After talking to the doctor on Tuesday and telling him I did not feel good, he said just wait until my appointment on Thursday for my 32-week checkup. When Tony came home, I told him I did not feel well, so he went to the Lamaze class alone.

My water broke before my Thursday appointment. The twins were coming two months early. We arrived at the small community hospital and were told of a really unusual situation. We had to take an ambulance to the Children's Hospital of Orange County (CHOC), which was 30 miles north of our home. There was another mom, 32 weeks pregnant with twins and she had a son at home, like we did. They were the same age. Her name was Adell, and mine was Idell. The coincidence was very uncanny, and we became fast friends. When I arrived at CHOC, the trauma began.

Two amniotic fluid samples were taken and returned. The long needle inserted twice in my stomach was disconcerting. My twins had lungs that were developed enough to allow them to survive outside the womb. Adell's twins were much bigger, but their lungs could not sustain them outside the womb. They held off the delivery of Adell's twins with drugs. She grew very big and told me she wanted to have her babies. She cried often when I went to see her while I was in the hospital.

The next three days were a whirl. I was given the option to deliver naturally as the twins were positioned correctly in the birthing canal. One of my twins was in distress, however, and might not have made the birthing process I was told. I chose the C-section to protect the babies. It was a long wait with much prayer outside the delivery/surgery room. I felt alone and was alone. Tony was at home, and we had no family near us.

The anesthesiologist was a very nice man. I had chosen a saddle block so I could be awake for the birth. He talked to me as I was very curious about the stages of a C-section.

"The noise you hear is the initial cut."

"Now the doctor is cutting the muscle."

He finally said, "Congratulations, Mrs. Koury! You just gave birth to twin sons!" One I got to hold and kiss at birth; the other was rushed to the Neonatal Intensive Care Unit (NICU) for treatment.

In recovery and that night, I was in excruciating pain. I had not prepared for a C-section and had chosen to be in the ward for normal deliveries. The nurses and new moms came into my room (sectioned by a sliding curtain) all night. I do not think the nurse realized that I had a C-section and was nearly cut in half. I begged for pain medicine after I was reluctant to take it because I was going to nurse my twins.

That night in all my stupor, I received a phone call from Dr. Amalie, the head of the CHOC NICU. He said that Twin B had only a 25% chance of survival. I prayed and cried. How could God give me twins and allow me to carry them only to take one back? I was confused and in pain. The next day, on a Thursday, Dr. Amalie called again and said, "Congratulations! Twin B survived the night and now has a 50% chance of surviving. Each night he survives, he has an increased chance of making it." I thanked God and continued to pray.

Dr. Amalie called early Friday morning. "Twin B survived the night and will probably make it. He needs a name." I did not tell him that the CHOC social worker had come by the day before to tell me that Koury Twin A and Koury Twin B needed a name. Tony and I prayed. We wanted biblical and twin names. At the same time, we said, "Andrew and Matthew." We told Dr. Amalie we selected names and that we had not named them before because we believed we would lose one of the twins. We believed he would die.

Tony came to my hospital room two days later. He stopped by my bed and sobbed. I felt like jumping out the window. I just knew he was crying because Twin B died. He calmed me down and explained that he was crying because he was touched by the personal care the nurses at the NICU were giving our sons. The nurses touched and sang to our twins 24/7. Tony was so touched by the love they received from the nurses that he just sobbed.

Dr. Amalie, the doctor who had spoken to me on the phone for the two nights before and the lead doctor at CHOC, showed up to my room later that day. He asked for Mrs. Koury. Recognizing his voice and expecting the worst news, I said, "I am Mrs. Koury." Dr. Amalie immediately put two Polaroid pictures in my face.

He said, "Mrs. Koury, meet your twin sons!" I did not see the IV connections or the breathing tube on Twin B. I just saw my beautiful son. I had seen Twin A at birth, but he looked healthy and bigger in the NICU bassinet.

I never left their side for the two weeks I was in the hospital. The medical staff would not let me leave as I was on antibiotics for an unknown infection. I was required to wash my hands and change before I touched, talked, and sang to the twins through the bassinet. I missed my oldest son at home. I begged the staff to let me go home after two weeks. They relented and sent me home with antibiotics.

Then the trek to the hospital, thirty miles north, began. It was first to see both twins, then to see only Twin B, or Matthew, as he stayed at CHOC for two months. One time, when Matt was in the hospital, Tony was stopped on El Toro Road while making a breast milk run to CHOC. The officer told him that a pedestrian stepped off the curb seven lanes over. In California, pedestrians had the right of way, and Tony would be ticketed. Tony tried to explain that he was on a milk run before he went to work and did not have time for a ticket. The officer gave him one anyway.

Another time when I came downstairs to take my middle-of-the-night feeding, I noticed that Tony, always trying to be practical, had propped the twins up with pillows on the sofa. He had the bottles in their mouths and was feeding them as he hung his head and slept. I screamed when I saw the sight. I knew they needed skin-to-skin contact for bonding, and he was supposed to hug each one.

The next eight months were a blur. I ended up in the hospital as I collapsed from exhaustion. I was determined to love and feed my twins breast milk to give them the immunity they needed. When I was not feeding, changing, or bonding with a son, I was in the downstairs bathroom pumping. The machine was rented for $50 a month. We did not have the money as our salary was cut in half when we moved to California. The cost of living was higher in the Golden State. We lived on rice, beans, and vegetables during our first year. My only clothes were from the secondhand store. I substituted while pregnant with TJ to bring in more money until I received a part-time job in Irvine, California. We did not have the money to pay for the pump, but we sacrificed for our sons. We never went out for entertainment or food. During that time, I learned much about my dependence on God, His love for us, and His provision after we submitted to His will.

Parenting three babies in diapers was hard. When I was an Early Childhood minor at UNM, I studied babies being formed in the womb from zygote to fetus. I taught young children and knew the stages of development. Parenting was still very hard.

I had studied the types of abortion available after Roe v. Wade was decreed the law of the land by the Supreme Court in 1973. Although I had no religious convictions against abortion, I remember feeling pity for the dependent baby extracted in pieces or born red as a result of a saline abortion. I thought to myself, *Isn't this murder? Aren't these vulnerable, dependent humans in a mother's womb? Aren't these babies tiny human beings?* I did not voice my thoughts when watching films of abortions.

I remember the disgust I felt, however, but tried to reason that it was the law that a baby could be dismembered or burned. I try to be logical. I knew babies from conception to early childhood. I knew about abortions and was disgusted at the thought. Parenting was still hard. These young baby boys depended on me and Tony for survival. We wanted children. We knew we made a choice to make babies. Parenting was still hard.

I often wondered, *Doesn't a mom know she could produce another human when engaging in unprotected sex and not taking the birth control pill? How is this logical to make a vulnerable, dependent little human pay for the choices of two consenting adults?* It made little sense to me as I pondered. I said nothing in class, however. My classmates accepted the Supreme Court ruling. Who was I to question it? I just thought these thoughts to myself but with an uneasy feeling inside. Weren't the strong supposed to protect and care for the weak? My reasoning could not reconcile what I was watching. I personally knew how hard it was. I was holding tiny babies. They would die without my care. They were dependent for survival.

I cared for a one-pound fifteen-ounce twin boy. The nurses worked so hard to save him. We were giving up our lives for the growth and development of another human. The Gospel of Christ made sense to me. He was innocent, yet Jesus died for me. He chose sacrifice for me. He loved me and gave His life for me. That is what we were doing for our twins. Tony and I were sacrificing and giving to others so they would have life. The truth of the Gospel was practical. Love God and love others made sense to me.

While I pumped milk daily for five months, I studied a picture in our downstairs bathroom. I had purchased it at a garage sale when we moved to California. At the bottom was inscribed a Bible verse.

It said, "But seek first the kingdom of God and his righteousness, and all these things will be added to you." (Matt. 6:33 ESV)

I thought about this verse as I sat there listening to the whooshing sound. Did God come into my life because I was "seeking"? What did "his righteousness" mean? Was I supposed to seek his righteousness, too?

21

God's Provision

We knew it was going to be expensive to pay for my two-week stay, Andy's three-week stay, and Matthew's eight-week stay at the hospital. The financial adviser at CHOC left her card on the NICU bassinet. Tony finally called her and said we had good insurance through Michelin. The girl was kind and asked if he knew it was $600 daily.

She said, "It is $600 a day *per baby*." How could we pay for the premature birth of our sons? I had barely spent any money on our firstborn. We only purchased diapers. He never had formula as he went from breastmilk to the cup. I bought our clothes and toys cheaply at garage sales.

We did not have money. Our only entertainment was a small TV and a console record player. I bought record albums at the garage sales. There was a budding Christian-music industry in California. I liked the music of Keith Greene, Mylon Lefevre and Broken Heart, Andre Crouch, Carmen, and others. I bought their used large albums and listened to their music daily. I learned about God and His principles by listening to these music artists. I learned that God loves me, will teach me His ways, and will provide for me. All He asked for was faith in Him. I put my faith in God, and He worked great miracles.

The first area I put my faith to work was financial. During the our hospital stay, we accrued a hospital bill of over $140,000. We did not have the money to pay. Thankfully, the insurance through Michelin just capped the annual cost to every covered employee.

Additionally, the state of California paid part of the hospital costs if our sons were born with hyalin membrane (underdeveloped lungs) at birth. We ended up paying $5,000 out of $140,000. God had shown up and provided for our finances. We had witnessed this provision with the returned cancellation letter when we trusted God with our finances. Here it was again.

The second provision came in the way of protection. God sent our neighbor John to live next to us. He was a member of the Hell's Angels Motorcycle Club. For some reason, John liked us. He told his motorcycle gang that they could not say any bad words around me. He once cussed out his dog in my presence. When I commented, "Pardon me?", John said, "No, not you! I didn't see you there. I was talking to my dog."

We both laughed. John's friends obeyed him. They were a mean-looking bunch of bikers but treated me with great respect. John worked on a construction site and would push his motorcycle to the corner early in the morning so as to not wake me or the babies.

At one point during the three years we lived on Via Robles in Mission Viejo, a car raced by our condominium and made noise in the middle of the night. When it happened for multiple nights in a row, Tony asked John if it was one of his friends who was waking me and our newborn sons up at night. John replied that it was not but wanted to be notified when the noise happened again. When it did, Tony told John. John took off running after the car, kicked in the door, and walked back up the hill. He had a girl hanging on his arm. When Tony looked at him puzzled, John explained that the only way to stop a hoodlum like that was to damage his car and take his girl. John said, "That will teach him. He won't bother you again." He did not ever come back. I felt strangely safe having a member of a motorcycle gang as a neighbor. God provided protection for us in a strange way, but I knew John was sent to live near us in California. I was learning to just trust.

The third instance of provision came in the form of food. We could not afford nutritious food that I required to eat healthy daily. At about that time, our church, Grace Community Church, bought a plot of land to build a new church. The land was full of orange trees. Our pastor asked for his congregation to pick as many oranges as we wanted before the grove was leveled to build a new church. We ate free and nutritious oranges and orange juice for months. We started to recognize God's provision, protection, and healthy substance when we could not afford it for ourselves. There was a pattern starting to be most evident. God was taking care of His own.

22

Spirits and Maryland

Tony announced that Michelin was promoting him and transferring him. He would begin his new job as district manager for the Baltimore District in January. This announcement came only eight months after the twins were born, and I went into full panic mode. He could not leave me alone while he found a house and set up a house in Maryland. I was independent but knew I could not pack alone and take care of three babies. I had been hospitalized with exhaustion recently. After Tony said we would move, I went to see a counselor. The counselor said the top three reasons for stress were the death of a loved one, a move to a new location, and the birth of a child. I had two of the three facing me and knew I could not be left alone with three small boys in diapers. I knew I couldn't be alone while Tony house-hunted.

My only request to Tony when he went alone to house-hunt was to find a place near Jack and Jackie Devine. They were Michelin friends who hosted pig roasts for the Michelin team when we lived in the DC area. They had children of their own, and Jackie's mom lived with them. They were good Catholics and had common sense. Jack, also, was an entertainer in his previous life. He made us laugh with his stories. I liked the Devines and wanted to live near them. They knew Michelin, children, and the area.

Tony bought a house in a snowstorm. I never saw it. He bought one near the Devine family in Ellicott City, Maryland. It was near Baltimore. He sent me and the three sons to live in Pennsylvania with his mom. He and his younger brother, George, moved us into the new home. I never packed a box, and I moved into a ready-to-live-in house in Maryland. My stay with Tony's mom in Pennsylvania was eventful and memorable. Sue and her new baby, Angel, also came to stay with Tony's mom during our stay. I continued to learn about the spiritual world from Sue. She had much experience and shared her stories with me.

Sue had been a hippie as a teenager. She once hitch-hiked and lived in a commune with love and peace children (or other hippies). She got saved and changed her appearance and life but had many stories to tell about her days before salvation. The spaced-out drug scene and her artistic ability fascinated me. We spent many hours talking through the night. Sue told me that she drew many pieces of art when she was unsaved. She had given her art to Tony but warned me that I should burn them. She was under demonic possession when she drew them. I was a new Christian and did not believe all she told me. I had to figure out life based on reason, evidence, and experience.

When we moved to California after our marriage, I wanted to decorate our new condominium. We used a used orange-and-brown tweed sofa. Above it, I placed a picture that Sue had drawn years before. All of Tony's family had warned me not to use that picture. It was drawn when Sue was in the occult. I thought it was religious hocus pocus. Afterall, it was a picture of blowing fall leaves and matched my sofa perfectly. It was an inanimate picture after all. Their warnings were ignored as I thought they were just being superstitious or "too religious." I hung the painting above the sofa and never thought about it for many months until something happened to me one day.

I laid down on the sofa downstairs as I had just delivered our oldest son a few weeks earlier. All of a sudden, I felt like a pillow was holding me down. I tried to move and could not. I thought I was becoming paralyzed after delivering our son. It did not make sense as I was just moving around the condominium. I felt fine but knew I needed to rest when the baby slept. I tried to make logical sense of the "paralysis." I remember looking at the picture hanging above the sofa. I stared at it and knew the paralysis had something to do with it. I was relatively new to this spiritual truth but remembered my mother-in-law telling me that the spoken word of God was like a sword of the spirit. I knew I had to fight whatever this was that was holding me down. I mumbled the only Bible verses I had memorized. I said the "Our Father" and repeated over and over, "Greater is He that is within me than He that is in the world" (1 John 4:4). As I repeated these verses over and over, the paralysis started to leave me. There was definitely a connection between my prayers and the paralysis. I experienced it. I knew it.

When I was completely mobile again, I ran upstairs to my mother-in-law and told her about what had just happened. She told me she would pray and ask God to reveal what happened. I fell asleep next to her. When I awoke a few minutes later, I described the unusual dream I just had. I told her that I was saying goodbye to seven critters who were smiling at me while waving. They were all in a large vehicle that looked like a Land Rover. My mother-in-law told me that there were seven demons waving good-bye to me. She said I should get rid of the picture Sue painted while she was in the occult. I did so right away. Not many choose to believe this story, so I do not share it often. I know this really happened to me and have devoted myself to learning about the spiritual world—God's messengers and Satan's messengers. I know that they are real. There is a spiritual world around us. We cannot see it, only feel the effects through people and events. To deny this truth is to deny reality. I experienced it. It was real. Others with me witnessed this truth. God revealed this truth over and over when we moved as a result of Michelin transfers and lived in Maryland and later in South Carolina.

There were other stories that I learned from Sue. She was an incredible person who was used by God in a mighty way. She and her husband, Steve, became ministers and ran a pro-life ministry in Aurora, Illinois. The prostitutes, drug addicts, and other needy women came off the streets, gave up their addiction, and learned to be productive and disciplined people at the home run by Sue and Steve. The women carried their babies and learned to care for their babies before and after birth.

Oprah Winfrey asked Sue about her ministry once when Oprah was airing her show. Sue was sitting in the audience of the popular talk show. Sue talked about her home for unwed mothers outside Chicago, Illinois, called Resurrection Life Ministry. She received thousands of donations after speaking about her ministry for only a few minutes. She received calls from around the country. God used Sue to care for others and to teach me and others His practical truth. He also revealed to me how many people are influenced by Oprah. How many people watch TV? It was eye-opening.

23

Filling Our Home

After Tony found a home, we finally moved into our new home on Carillon Drive in Ellicott City, Maryland, thanks to Tony and his younger brother, George, who helped with the transition. The three babies and I went from California to Pennsylvania to Maryland. I went from home to home.

Jack and Jackie came to our front door a few weeks later and announced, "We are here to watch your sons. Go shopping for your home."

We looked at each other and said, "We don't leave our sons with sitters."

The only time we did that in California, our two neighbors came over for two hours when the twins were five months old. They were eager for us to return and announced that they did not know how we took care of three babies. My mother-in-law, Imee, told me often that no one would ever believe what we did to care for three sons.

The Devines were insistent. They asked us frequently on phone calls during that day, "Did you purchase curtains, throw rugs, and linen?" If we replied that we had not, yet, they said, "Do not come home until you do."

We shopped all day and did not shop again for curtains, rugs, and linen for the seven years we lived in Maryland. We frequently thought about God blocking the cancellation letter which allowed us to purchase a condominium in California and a house to live in Maryland. I did not work outside the home to supplement our income, but God was still providing for us.

We decided to buy furniture for our formal living room and dining room after a child remarked that we had set up a "real haunted house" when they came to our house around Halloween. We had been in the house for almost two years but did not have the time or money to buy furniture—until that comment.

We then made the time and looked for furniture. We still have the furniture we bought in 1983. They are in our reading and dining rooms. I am sitting on a French Provincial wingback chair and staring at the French Provincial loveseat we bought then. I still love them.

Life in Maryland taught me much about children, public education, and politics. My neighbor sent her children to a private school. It was hard for me to understand this decision. I graduated from a large public school and graduated from the University of New Mexico—a public university. I taught in the Albuquerque public schools and never considered sending our sons to a private school. They would take the bus to school with all the neighborhood children and hang out with their school friends after school. The boys attended a private preschool and a private kindergarten, but they were definitely going to transfer to Centennial Elementary School after their preschool years because I was a strong public elementary school advocate.

Tony faced many challenges at Michelin during this period. He was invited to be in charge of any country in Europe. His reply to the international recruiter was he would go to any English-speaking country offered. The Michelin international recruiter closed his notebook and left the building. Tony immediately knew that was not the answer the recruiter wanted to hear. Tony was to learn another language.

Michelin then decided to place Tony on probation because he exercised mercy on an employee who had been drinking. Tony knew the employee had a family and exercised leniency to the young man and gave him a warning. Michelin, at that time, did not put people on probation to remediate them. It was a nice way to tell the employee, "Use this time to find another job." We knew that and were distraught at the possibility because I was not working, we had three young sons, and we had a mortgage to pay. We decided to give our latest challenge to God and just pray about it.

We saw Tony little during those months, but we knew he was working hard for us. I kept busy during the summer months as our sons were on the St. John's Lane Dive and Swim Teams. It was our only extracurricular. During the times they were not at preschool or at practice, we went to the neighborhood park or played with the neighborhood children.

We were good friends with Laurie, a Jewish neighbor who had three preschool girls about the ages of our three sons. We shared Jewish and

Christian holidays to expose our children to the other religion and to educate them. Laurie will always be one of my favorite friends.

About this time, we found out that the Jeremiah People, a Christian performing group, were going to perform the musical *Joseph and the Amazing Technicolor Dreamcoat* at Centennial public high school down the street. We attended the musical. We knew after we saw the musical that God was speaking to us through this musical play at a secular school about a biblical character. A refrain in one of the songs was, "When God closes a door, He opens a window." We knew that song and that line were for us. Tony believed that God was closing a door but opening a window.

Tony was never taken off of probation or let go. As a matter of fact, the man who had put Tony on probation had to get Tony's permission to sell government tires in one area. The story was just like the biblical Joseph. His brothers had sold him but later had to ask for Joseph's permission. God was taking care of us, and we knew it. Tony never lost his job and was honored for his work a few years later.

24

Centennial and Truth

Our oldest son was enrolled in kindergarten at Centennial Public Elementary School. I volunteered to be the room mother. One of my responsibilities was to plan for class parties. I met with Ms. Prince, the kindergarten teacher, and asked if I should plan a Christmas party.

She looked at me with surprise and said, "Mrs. Koury, we do not celebrate Christmas in the public schools." I looked at her with equal surprise and she said, "You know, separation of church and state."

But, I thought, we celebrated Christmas in the public schools when I attended and taught there about ten years before. I was confused as to what had changed, but I was relatively new to Maryland and the school life as a parent. I did not want to create problems.

"Okay," I proceeded to ask Ms. Prince, "for what parties should I plan? Easter? Valentine's Day?"

She stopped me again and said, "We do not celebrate Easter in the public schools. You remember? Separation of church and state?"

I was not going to argue, but I was still confused. "For what parties should I plan?"

Ms. Prince replied, "You should plan for a Halloween party and a Valentine's party."

With confusion and surprise, I asked her, "Do you mean St. Valentine's Day?" Ms. Prince just looked pensively at me.

I was determined to raise our sons differently than the way we were raised. I was going to be involved in our son's life. A little boy named Ben stole our son's Show and Tell weekly. This was before e-mail and easy communication. When Ben repeatedly stole our son's toy, I wanted to go to see Mrs. Chidester, our son's first-grade teacher. However, parents were not allowed in the classroom until October. When the month arrived, I asked Ms. Chidester about the stolen items. Her response was, "That is what your son said." When I told her the toys that he took to school never came home, she said she did not see them, so she couldn't accuse Ben. When I asked her if they have rules in her class, like not stealing, not lying, or not hitting, her reply surprised me.

Ms. Chidester said, "We do not teach values in the public schools. We get the students the way they come to us. We do not try to change them. What your son said is based on values. We do not teach values!"

I was surprised at her response. When students leave the classroom, they would be arrested for the violation of these values. I was confused. Did we stop teaching good citizenship? I found out that Ben burned down his house years later. I guess he was allowed to live out his own values. Ben had my sympathy as he was adopted a few months before. Freedom to do whatever he wanted was not freedom to me, however. It was bondage to impulse or desire. Ben gave into impulse, and I do not know what ever happened to him.

The issue with not teaching values in public school appeared in other aspects of our son's life. One day, he came running into the house, holding his private parts and asking me what a "scrotum" was. I had not been prepared to give the talk about the "birds and the bees" to a second-grader. I calmly sat him down and explained what a scrotum was.

He asked other questions about what he heard at the table from girls who had older sisters. My thought was the kids at that table had lost their innocence too young. Students that age should be protected from ideas they are not old enough to comprehend. I was sad and angry that I had to explain things to an eight-year-old. The omission of teaching values in the public schools was starting to take its toll on my family. I did not want to live in a valueless culture. I knew we could not survive as a family, neighborhood, state, and nation. Every law and every rule is based on someone's values.

I hated the atheistic Communism. It taught the "values" of the state. I lived through the confusion of Cold War ideas. When the former governor of California, Ronald Reagan, won the Republican nomination for the presidency in 1980, I watched his strongly anti-Communist policies during his first term. I became a strong Reagan supporter when he called the Union of Soviet Socialist Republics (USSR) the "evil empire." I joined the Moral Majority and became a vocal supporter.

It was reason and personal experience that led me to support Reagan. He was not perfect, but he, along with Margaret Thatcher, caused the disintegration of the "evil empire." My personal experience caused me to believe there was evil in the world. I believe now that Adolph Hitler was influenced by evil forces. There were many others throughout history who devalued human life and mutilated and murdered people, including the crazy Roman Emperor Caligula, Pol Pot, Josef Stalin, and others. I believe that the fall of the last Christian Czar of Russia was largely due to the evil mystic Rasputin.

The last Christian Czar, Nicholas Romanov and his family were murdered after Russia fell to Leninism (a form of Marxism/Communism). Joseph Stalin replaced Lenin and the USSR gained strength.

I find it coincidental that one evil man, Stalin, was betrayed by someone just as evil. Hitler betrayed Stalin when he ignored the Non-Aggression Pact during World War II. They were both evil and totalitarian. Stalin, when he finally came out of his self-pitying stupor, became a western ally out of his vengeance.

Winston Churchill knew Stalin was not to be trusted. Ronald Reagan called the USSR "the evil empire." Ronald Reagan was on to something. We do not battle against flesh and blood but against powers and principalities in high places. I wanted to help Reagan gain victory for a second term. I worked hard through much opposition in a Reagan-hating Maryland but was fully committed.

My passion for activism was spurred by my personal experience and the ability to reason. Our son was forced to pray with a Christian friend in secrecy in the Centennial Elementary schoolyard. I knew the Bill of Rights. I was troubled as to why the "free exercise" of religion was not protected. I knew that the rights of the people had to be explicitly protected for the U.S. Constitution to be ratified. Why did my son have to hide to pray? Where was the protection by state entities? I did not want to stir things, but I knew this was against the U.S. Constitution.

When our son was in Mrs. Grimes' class, I requested to give a social studies lesson on the season called Winter Break. I asked the students if they knew why we were off of school for two weeks. I asked them if they knew why we exchanged gifts. I asked them why they see stars, shepherds, and stargazers. I then asked them if they knew what a crèche was, or if they knew who the baby in the manger was.

Overwhelmingly, the students did not know the answers to these questions. Maybe it was my Catholic upbringing or the fact that most of my public-school students knew the answers to these questions in New Mexico, but I was sincerely shocked that the students did not know the history behind our U.S. traditions. Christmas is a federal holiday and the most commercial day of the year. The students did not know why. I was shocked and knew I had to do something about it.

25

Activism

I **knew I had to do something about students not knowing fun-**
damental history.

In Maryland we attended Chapelgate Presbyterian Church. They
had organized programs for our sons. During the summers of 1984-1986, I
volunteered to help with Vacation Bible School (VBS). Tony and I were also
mentored by the director of middle schools in Howard County. His name
was Dr. DiVirgilio, and he was a man of God. He also attended Chapelgate
and led our small group. We attended his Bible Study and learned much
about God. I also attended a prayer meeting with Catholics every week. I
was hungry for spiritual truth and was thirsty for knowledge.

When I told my Bible study that I wanted to teach about Christmas
traditions to our community, they agreed to help and pray about it. When
I told the Catholic women's prayer group about my plan, they were incred-
ibly supportive. It really wasn't "my plan." It was given to me in a vision
in the middle of the night. God had started to speak to me in visions. I knew
it was Him but felt I could not tell anyone.

Tony was startled when I woke him up and told him I was supposed
to direct a Christmas pageant at a local public high school to educate the
community about the meaning of Christmas. God had revealed His plan to
me in a vision. After Tony was fully awake and calm, he asked, "What
makes you think you are supposed to do that?"

I told him that God had told me in a dream and I had a choice to believe and obey or not. Tony thought about it and agreed to help me. He
sensed the urgency in my voice and knew it was not my own idea.

Susan, my dear friend, helped me with preparations for the play God
told me I was to direct. I directed the pageant for three years at a local public high school. Our sons played parts in my play, and original music was

written and sung for it. We made props and had tryouts. The cast was young students.

Over 500 people attended the play every year at Howard High School. It was a great success, and I was obedient to my calling. I knew that God would make a way if I were just obedient. I was, and He made a way to educate so many residents of Howard County, Maryland. Our convictions were confirmed by our experiences in Maryland.

Our sons went to Centennial Elementary School during the school year. We learned why our sons were not being taught values in school. The principal of Centennial Lane Elementary School, Mr. Mitchell, met us at the cafeteria door as we entered our first Parent Teacher (PTA) Night. Tony stood up and asked if values are ever taught in the classroom.

Mr. Mitchell retorted to Tony, "We do not teach values in the public schools! You teach your kids at home, and we will teach them their academics at school."

While I tried to understand his strong opinion, I was confused. There were rules to be followed in a civil society. We would experience chaos if everyone did what was right in their own eyes. There were laws to be followed. It was the purpose of education to educate. Besides that, the Howard County public schools observed Yom Kipper, Sukkot, Diwali, Muslim holidays, and other eastern religious holidays. On which none of our U.S. laws are based, but they were clearly religious. I was disturbed by the double standard.

My activism increased after these experiences. All should be taught in school. Why were some holidays not taught and others were taught?

We had worked on a campaign to have our Christian voice on the Howard County School Board. Later when we moved to South Carolina, I was told by one of my friends in Maryland that they had elected another conservative Christian to the school board. Another one was elected after we moved. I was told that "values education" was going to be taught in the Howard County Public Schools. My friends knew our passion and support for this policy. Not only had we told them about the experience with our oldest son, Ben, and Mrs. Chidester, but we also told our friends about the PTA meeting attended by Tony. They knew this news would be welcomed.

26

Signs and Wonders

God showed Himself as an answerer of prayers. There were so many miraculous events in Maryland.

Janice, our neighbor, was an occasional babysitter for our three sons when we lived in Maryland. One day, I told Janice about my spiritual experiences that led me to a new faith in Christ alone. She was from the area and had never heard about Jesus. I told her it was a spiritual matter, and she could cognitively confess her distance from God and believe that God sent his only Son into the world as a human to bridge the gap between man and God.

I told Janice that Jesus was sent to the earth so that we could spiritually live in eternity just by accepting Him into our hearts. All she had to do was acknowledge Jesus, confess, and ask Jesus into her heart as the Holy Spirit.

Janice agreed and wanted to say the prayer above. She did. When her eyes opened, she said, "Mrs. Koury, I have a problem believing anything happened." Knowing the story of Abraham and Gideon who both boldly asked God for intervention, I prayed and asked God for a sign to show us that what Janice prayed was real.

We opened our eyes, and there was a white dove sitting on the rail on our deck just staring at us. I knew in my spirit that it was the sign I had asked for. It was a sign of the Holy Spirit. Janice went home and told her mom, Kerry, about what had happened.

Kerry came to our house a short time later and wanted to hear about the story I told her daughter, Janice. I told Kerry the same account. She opened her eyes after she tearfully asked Jesus into her heart.

She said, "I need to know this is true. I do not have your faith." I apologized to God but boldly prayed and asked God for a sign. We opened our eyes to a staring white dove on the banister on our deck. I knew it was a sign from the Lord that He heard and answered my prayer.

There are no coincidences in the Lord when you come to Him, acknowledge Him as Lord, and pray to Him, believing that He hears you. The same staring white dove was a sign from God for both Janice and Kerry. We all knew it was an answer to our prayer.

Our neighbors in Maryland knew of our zealous and growing faith in God. We prayed about everything. When neighbors asked Tony to join them in their latest "barn raising," the neighbors offered to bring the beer. Tony told them not to worry about bringing beer for him. They looked surprised and replied, "You will be drinking with the rest of us by the end of the summer."

Tony then responded, "Either I will be drinking, or you will not by the end of the summer." It so happened that, because of health and other issues, none of the guys were drinking by summer's end.

The neighbors had ended their drinking but not their practical jokes. Once we went to New Mexico to visit my family for two weeks. Before we left, we had to tell the neighbors about our very fertile soil behind our house. The seeds we had planted only weeks before had already sprouted and were visible through the soil. We told this story to them as we asked for them to take turns and water our garden while we were away.

When we returned late at night after two weeks away, we took a flashlight and wanted to see the growth. Neither of us had planted a garden before and were interested in how much it had grown in our absence. After all, we had seen incredible growth before we left. Our soil was certainly fertile.

What we saw shocked us, and we could not wait to tell the neighbors. There were full-grown tomato, corn, pepper, and cucumber plants. Not only were the plants full-grown, but they also had full-grown vegetables on them! We were very impressed by our fertile soil and were eager to tell our neighbors about it. We had a late-night visitor, however. He changed everything.

At our door the next night was our neighbor and local dentist. Lew told us he could not go on vacation the next day without a clear conscience, so he told us the truth. He sheepishly started with, "That is not your garden."

We looked surprised and he repeated, "That is not your garden."

He then told us the truth. Lew was credible because he had grown his own garden and knew the process of gardening. Lew told us that the neighbors had visited a full-grown garden nearby at night and dug up the full-grown plants and replanted them in our garden while we were gone. We listened with surprise, disbelief, and confusion.

"How" we asked, "could replanted crops produce vegetables?"

Lew replied, "They are not your vegetables!" Now we were really puzzled and glad our sons were sleeping.

"What do you mean, 'Not your vegetables?'"

He proceeded to say, "That is not your garden, plants, nor vegetables. The neighbors decided to play a practical joke on you after you told us how fertile your soil was. Some of the guys went to nearby gardens and dug up and replanted the plants. Then we used tape or just propped up the full-grown vegetables to make it appear that they had grown while you were gone."

Tony and I felt humored but devised a plan anyway. We went to see our neighbors after Lew's visit. One by one, they were too busy to hear our story, or they told us they were going out and could not listen. Tony, knowing the truth at this point, said public things like:

"Were the neighbors upset that we were gone for two weeks?"

"Did they resent having to water our vegetable garden?"

"Were they just jealous that we had such success as novices in gardening?"

We had great neighbors. We disagreed politically and religiously but genuinely loved each other. Why were they acting so aloof at our "good news"? We knew they were hiding the truth but played along with them. Lew had told us the truth.

Tony told the neighbors that the University of Maryland (UMD) Agricultural Extension Service was sending workers the next week to take soil samples to determine why our soil was so fertile as to produce full-grown plants and vegetables to pick and eat after only two weeks. As Tony went on rambling that maybe our garden would make the newsletter for our rich soil, our neighbor, Kathy told her son, Robert, "Go get your dad." Robert ran up the hill when Tony was in mid-sentence.

Kathy exclaimed to us with urgency, "That is not your garden!"

Tony played along with them and replied, totally ignoring their claim, "Did Robert tell you that the UMD Agricultural Extension Service is sending someone out to take a sample of our rich soil?"

The women screamed, "They can't! The garden is not yours!" They proceeded to tell us what Lew already confessed a week before.

When Tony's expression turned to pretend anger, I intervened to stop the charade as I saw the expression on the women's faces. Tony had told them "angrily" that his professional career was on the line as he told the UMD Ag Extension Office that we had rich soil. He was going to have to call them and ask them not to come.

The neighbors found out about Lew's midnight confession over 25 years later when the neighbors had a get-together, and Tony dropped in to see them. They did not know that Lew told us the truth the night after we returned. They believed our story for years.

Tony and I decided to join in on the practical jokes. One time, we all knew about a black flag with a tooth on it to humor our flag-waving dentist friend, Lew. We attended a picnic at Lew's. He had no idea we had raised that black flag until he looked up while eating in his backyard. His expression was hilarious.

Another time we showed up at our neighbor's house as the "upside-down people." Tony and I put balloons between our legs, put sunglasses and hats on the balloons, and walked slowly to the house next door. Our neighbor, Chuck, looked at us with astonishment when he opened the door. He proceeded to welcome us as he bent over and talked to our balloon heads. Our actual heads were covered with our pants, so Chuck really thought we were upside down.

Yet another time, Leslie, Chuck's wife put pictures in Chuck's suitcase for him to see once he opened his suitcase in Europe. Chuck drank alcohol much and would pass out and not recall the night before. Chuck was on the front lines in Vietnam as a medic and got drunk often to block out what he saw in Vietnam.

Leslie decided to play a practical joke on him and arranged for women to come to her house and take a photo under the covers of Chuck and Leslie's bed. It was an attempt to get Chuck to stop drinking until he passed out with no memory of the night before. It worked. He saw the pictures when he was sober. He saw himself and the neighborhood women in his bed. It scared him, and he stopped drinking so heavily after the joke was played on him.

27

Daddy Dies

Daddy had left Zura and was back in Albuquerque. He had lived with my sister while in Texas to care for her sons in between her marriages. He left there and lived in a hotel for a while, then came to live with my mom on Morris Street in Albuquerque. I had moved my younger sister, Sylvia, and my mom after Badu came back into my mom's and sister's life. I did not like the drunk and did not want him near my mom and sister.

My mom easily accepted my dad when he asked her if he could come live with her on Morris Street. She was kind and loving. She took care of him after he had heart troubles and was hospitalized. She wrote to me often and told me she was happy with my dad.

My mom called me. She said I needed to come home right away. I insisted that she ask the three evangelists she told me about to come over when I flew home. I recorded them and still possess their story. My mom said she would. I flew to Albuquerque after I told my family what my mom had told me on the phone.

Momma recounted this story on the phone, it was confirmed by three visitors, and I have their firsthand account on a cassette tape. My mom said she had gone out to buy something at the store. She left and three "visitors" came to the door. Daddy struggled to open it as he had stopped taking his Coumadin and all the other medicines he kept in a shoe box.

Daddy answered the door and greeted the three strangers. The two ladies and a man told Daddy that they were traveling evangelists and were just in Albuquerque for a few days. The women and the man told Daddy that God had said there was a very sick man at 514 Morris and that they should go visit with him.

My dad was a very outgoing and gregarious person. It was unusual for him not to welcome the visitors into Mom's apartment. He told the visitors he was a very sick man and could not invite them in to talk.

My daddy was in no condition to entertain three strangers. From what I learned and from firsthand accounts, the discussion went back and forth. The evangelists insisted they had to be obedient to God's voice, and my dad insisted that he was too sick to let them come in.

When my mom returned from the store, the three evangelists were inside praying over my dad as they laid hands on him.

Daddy died that night.

I know that God heard my prayers, spoke to three strangers just visiting Albuquerque, and I will see my daddy again in Heaven. The evangelists told me in person and on recorded tape about my daddy accepting Jesus into his heart that day. He was sincere, and they were obedient to God's voice. My daddy never had the abundant life here on earth because he would not surrender his life to the Lord's calling, but I know beyond a shadow of a doubt that I will see him in Heaven. All this is recorded for unbelievers to hear their accounts.

My mom had no funds to pay for a service, casket, or plot. My generous husband paid for everything. Daddy's graveside memorial was attended by only a few people. Afterwards, we went back to my mom's apartment. We spent three days as she cried and told me about her sexual abuse by her cousins and their friends. My mom was raw emotionally and shared emotions she had suppressed or covered with alcohol for many years. I understood her pain and suffering. I loved Momma for being honest and raw with her memories. I cried with her as she recounted her life.

My grandfather, Maximiliano Baca, owned a woodyard on Broadway Street. After my grandmother, Delfina Chavez Baca, was institutionalized when my mom was young, she spent time with her cousins and the Gurule family. It was during the hours between the end of school and my grandfather's arrival home from his woodyard that my mom was raped by her cousins and their friends. My mom recounted vivid details about the activities of her cousins and their friends. She told me that she never learned the correct response to a man and did not understand that courtship comes before sex. She was never instructed that sex was to be preserved until marriage. She, tearfully, accounted why she had multiple marriages and affairs. She told me repeatedly that Daddy was a good man and did not know what to do with Mom's philandering. She, tearfully, said she was sorry for her past and she drank to rid herself of the memories. For at least two days, she exposed her past pain. She said she had never told anyone about her past because it was too painful. I just listened and hugged her a lot. Now I understood why she had affairs, why we were placed in foster care, and why Daddy left often. I cried with Mom as I shared her pain.

During the three days that she revealed her painful memories for the first time, I told her that Jesus was more than just a religious figure. He was the Son of God. He came to be a bridge between man and God. He shed His blood as a sacrifice for all of our sins. He took our punishment. I told Mom that the just will live by this faith, belief, and spiritual truth (Rom. 1:17). All that Jesus requires is that we acknowledge, confess, repent, and invite His Spirit into our life. It was not religion. It was not rule-following. There were no organizational practices that should be kept. It was a simple acceptance of this spiritual truth as Jesus told a religious leader named Nicodemus in the Bible book of John, chapter 3.

> Now there was a Pharisee, a man named Nicodemus who was a member of the Jewish ruling council. He came to Jesus at night and said, "Rabbi, we know that you are a teacher who has come from God. For no one could perform the signs you are doing if God were not with him."
>
> Jesus replied, "Very truly I tell you, no one can see the kingdom of God unless they are born again."
>
> "How can someone be born when they are old?" Nicodemus asked. "Surely they cannot enter a second time into their mother's womb to be born!"
>
> Jesus answered, "Very truly I tell you, no one can enter the kingdom of God unless they are born of water and the Spirit. Flesh gives birth to flesh, but the Spirit gives birth to spirit. You should not be surprised at my saying, 'You must be born again.' The wind blows wherever it pleases. You hear its sound, but you cannot tell where it comes from or where it is going. So it is with everyone born of the Spirit."
>
> "How can this be?" Nicodemus asked.
>
> "You are Israel's teacher," said Jesus, "and do you not understand these things? Very truly I tell you, we speak of what we know, and we testify to what we have seen, but still you people do not accept our testimony. I have spoken to you of earthly things and you do not believe; how then will you

believe if I speak of heavenly things? [13] No one has ever gone into heaven except the one who came from heaven—the Son of Man. Just as Moses lifted up the snake in the wilderness, so the Son of Man must be lifted up, that everyone who believes may have eternal life in him.

"For God so loved the world that he gave his one and only Son, that whoever believes in him shall not perish but have eternal life. For God did not send his Son into the world to condemn the world, but to save the world through him. Whoever believes in him is not condemned, but whoever does not believe stands condemned already because they have not believed in the name of God's one and only Son. This is the verdict: Light has come into the world, but people loved darkness instead of light because their deeds were evil. Everyone who does evil hates the light, and will not come into the light for fear that their deeds will be exposed. But whoever lives by the truth comes into the light, so that it may be seen plainly that what they have done has been done in the sight of God." (NIV)

Momma wanted to be free from the bondage she was under. I told her that everything in her past was forgiven. It would be washed away. By just believing she could embrace a new life, She could be born again. Jesus would give her a new life.

Her transgressions would be removed as far as the east is from the west. She wanted this freedom. She wanted to have the joy of a new life. She accepted Christ as her personal Savior, not just a religious figure. Momma became a new person the day she accepted Christ. She was over 100 years old and talked about Christ to anyone who was willing to listen. God has restored what the locusts ate. She was a new person since that day over 35 years ago. Everyone around my mom knows this truth. My mom experienced the spiritual rebirth that Jesus talked about when he told Nicodemus about being born again.

She had a new life. She was full of thankfulness and joy. Her past was behind her. Sadly, some not only remember their past but live there. My mom could remember but not act out of her abuse. She could read about and act in God's ways. There is so much joy living in a new life. She experienced it.

28

South Carolina

Tony was recruited to work in advertising for Michelin Tire South Carolina. If he took the offer, it would mean a move to Michelin North America Headquarters in Greenville. Tony took the offer, and we made plans to move even though we loved Maryland.

One of my Catholic prayer group members was in real estate. We asked her to sell our house in Maryland. Since that returned cancellation letter when we knelt and asked God for His direction since we could not decide, we had made money on each sale. We were just following Michelin and asking God to direct us. He did. I always remember the Bible verse that says, "We receive not, because we ask not" (James 4:2-3). God knew the motives of our hearts and knew we did not want to move to get rich.

At first, I thought the listing price was too high. No other house in the neighborhood has sold for that much. Our realtor told me to just listen to my husband and let him set the price. I did as she said and just prayed. A few weeks after listing our house, we sold it for $50,000 more than any other house in the neighborhood. God was still directing our finances.

We knew we would miss our Maryland neighbors when we moved to South Carolina as a result of a Michelin offer. We knew that Jack and Jackie Devine had moved to South Carolina as a result of Jack's move with Michelin. We were looking forward to seeing them again. Our Maryland neighbors threw a going away picnic for us at a local park. We tearfully said goodbye to them. We loved Maryland, the Howard County Youth Programs, the Baltimore Orioles baseball games, the St. John Lane Dive and Swim Teams, the DiVirgilios, Tree Climbers, VBS, and all our friends at Chapelgate Presbyterian Church. We knew we had to move, but saying goodbye was hard for us. We decided to pack our bags and take our sons to Disney World as we awaited our temporary home in Greenville.

Shortly after we returned from our vacation, we moved into the temporary Huntington Apartments. We moved to South Carolina during the summer of 1989. Our three sons, all in elementary school, enjoyed playing near the man-made lakes in the apartment complex.

One day they "accidentally" hit a bird while they were skipping rocks on the lake. The bird fell into the lake. Our sons asked for me to help save the bird that they "accidentally" hit. I ran to the lake and got the bird out. The only place to keep the hurt bird was in our bathtub while we tried to contact animal rescue in Greenville. They took care of hurt animals. After several calls to animal rescue charities, I was referred to someone who took care of wounded birds, or "the bird lady" as she was called. She would help.

29

Hurricane Hugo and River Walk

When Tony came home from work, I told him that he could not use the downstairs bathroom. He asked, "Why not?" Then he proceeded to open the bathroom door and witness the bird droppings in the bathtub. He informed us that bird droppings carry disease. Fortunately for us and for the bird, the "bird lady" rescued the bird, and I cleaned the tub.

Hurricane Hugo hit South Carolina in late September. We had never lived anywhere that was in hurricane paths. I watched the path of the storm and knew it would hit the SC coastline and possibly spawn tornadoes near us. During the night, I watched the storm's path and moved our family downstairs as there were nearby tornadoes. We awoke to the devastation around us. It was particularly bad in the barrier islands. The next days and weeks revealed just how bad it had been. Never had I imagined we could die or be seriously injured as a result of a hurricane or tornado. There were estimates of over 50 people who died as a result of Hurricane Hugo in SC. Many more were injured. The storm was a rude welcome to the south.

Another event that caught my attention when we moved to SC was the political scandal called "Operation Lost Trust." The Federal Bureau of Investigation (FBI) investigated the South Carolina Legislature for illegal activities including drug use, bribery, and extortion. Most of the General Assembly who were indicted and convicted were Democrats. The scandal gave way to the control of the state legislature by Republicans. The investigation was over in 1999. Eighteen lawmakers were ultimately convicted. Three were Republicans. I was surprised when we moved to the Bible Belt. I thought we had moved to a safe and ethical place. We were not safe from hurricanes nor ethical violations I learned. The scandal gave way to ethics reform. I had time to reflect when I was not shopping for our new home. I learned that human nature was the same in the north, south, east, and west.

Our house in Riverwalk was finished that fall. Our three sons had enrolled at Southside Christian School (SCS) after my visit to the neighborhood public school. My plan was to enroll them in public education. I was in public school for middle and high school. I taught in a public school, and our sons went to the public schools in Maryland. I had changed my religious views, however. I found increasing hostility to our new faith in the public square. Being new to South Carolina, I did not want to create waves, so we enrolled our sons at SCS.

Months before, when looking for a home in South Carolina, I expressed the desire of my heart to live near Jack and Jackie Devine again. We had gone to their house months after they had moved to South Carolina. When we bought a lot of land to build a house, we did not know that we were buying a lot on the next street over from Jack and Jackie. I had thought of the Bible verse Psalm 37:4: "Delight yourself in the Lord and he will give you the desires of your heart" (ESV). God had done that so many times in the past, I do not know why I ever doubted this truth.

Our sons wanted to be friends with neighborhood children as they did in Maryland. They faced rejection because they attended that "Baptist school." For a year and a half, I told them to turn the other cheek and allow the neighbors to call them names and exclude them. After all, we were the Christians and had to be bigger than others who did not follow the law of love. The law of love includes patience, kindness, and self-control. We exercised that law for one-and-a-half years. We invited neighbors to birthday and sports teams' parties but still faced rejection because we went to a different school.

There is another verse that proclaims King David as a man after God's own heart. *But why?* I thought to myself. David was a warrior. Can a warrior be a person after God's heart? When the people of God were mocked and were fearful, David slew a giant. David did not have any fear. He had the faith that God would slay a giant if he was steadfast in his faith. I started to reevaluate my instructions to our sons. How could cowards be evangelists? Then I thought of another verse, 1 Corinthians 9:19-23. We are to be all things to all people for the sake of the gospel. So, I understood this truth. My instructions to our sons changed.

When we were gathered together, I instructed them that they would *never* cause a fight. They would *never* throw the first punch. But the new rules were that they could defend themselves if someone punched them first. My new instructions were tested shortly after they were given.

One of our sons was playing with a friend from SCS. Seven young men surrounded them and called them names. Our son rightly brought his friend inside. Our oldest son then went outside. The same seven young men surrounded him. One young man shoved him in the chest. Our son informed the young man that he was not allowed to hit anyone if they did not hit first as he was recently instructed.

The young man hauled off and hit our son. Our son defended himself and hit the young man back, It was just one punch, but the young man hit his head on the curve and landed in the hospital emergency room.

Our son ran into the open garage where I was standing. He was red in the face. He told me what happened moments before. I asked, "Who hit first?" He told me that the other guy did, and he defended himself. I said, "Okay, it is sad that it has come to this."

I had pleaded with two other moms to talk to their sons about pushing, teasing, or hitting our sons. I asked if we could just live in peace. I was told, "Boys will be boys, and they are to work out their own problems." All these words were running through my mind when I heard profanity being spewed from my driveway. What I witnessed shocked and angered me. These young men were calling for my son and waving sticks outside my house. I was hot and lost all my religion.
"You have the audacity to come to my home and threaten us with sticks?" I yelled. "You all better leave, or I'm going to take the sticks and use them on you!"

I was not exercising self-control nor was I acting in love. I was prepared to slay a giant when someone came down the street swinging arms and threatening me with words. Our encounter was not pretty. I understood later that she was upset that her son had to go to the hospital. I thought about how family and friends would call me a "chili pequin," or little hot pepper, when I was young. I felt awful that I lost my temper. I had committed to live a different life, and I lost my cool. I felt ashamed that I went back to my old ways.

Sue, Tony's sister, called from Chicago when I finally went inside. Sue said that I was under spiritual attack, and she wanted to pray for me. She may have been right. I acted in a way that was against what I wanted. I was in a spiritual battle. Sue prayed for me.

About two weeks after the incident, two of the boys involved were going to church activities with our sons. The mom who came after me in anger was a lane judge for the swim team and apologized to me profusely when she had to disqualify one of our sons. Her apology was more than I expected. We gained new friends the hard way in our new neighborhood in South Carolina.

30

The Campaign

SCS's tuition for three sons was expensive. When I was asked to teach for two hours in exchange for a discount on tuition, I accepted it. I met many wonderful parents and students as I taught two hours of history daily. I loved that we prayed and had devotions at SCS. Our sons now attended a school consistent with our views. They did not have to hide or face ridicule anymore. Most of the students and their parents believed like we did.

One of the families I met was the Hershey Family. They had moved here from Michigan. Julie Hershey was very knowledgeable about school matters and was an excellent speaker. I attended her presentation on Barney the purple dinosaur and other movements in education. I was very impressed by her knowledge of educational trends, and we became fast friends. She confirmed what I had experienced. She was right to inform and educate parents.

Julie attended a women's Christian political activity group. She called me one day to pray for her. The women in the group asked Julie to run for Greenville County (GC) School Board after being in Greenville only three months. She was to challenge a powerful GC school board member, Duke McCall from District 21 (now District 22). I agreed to pray, knowing that God can do the humanly "impossible." Julie had only been in Greenville County for a short time. Julie attended college but did not possess a SC teacher's certificate. Her children were in private not public schools because of school trends. Now she was going to run against the chairmen of the GC Board of Trustees? I agreed to pray anyway. I was going to trust God.

Julie called a few days after she agreed to run for Greenville County Greenville Trustee in November of 1991. She said that the group of ladies agreed that she should ask me to be her campaign manager because of my education and political experience. I attended one of their meetings and joined in their discussion. They persuaded Julie to call me. She did. I responded that I needed to pray and ask my husband. I voiced my concern that I was a private Christian school history teacher, and our three sons attended a Christian school. I only taught part-time but knew the campaign would be time-consuming. I agreed to pray about it.

Answers to prayer came from family, friends, and my employer. That fall I was moved to a Tot's Time Out (TTO) part-time position. I was not initially happy that I was moved from middle school to teaching four-year-olds in a church ministry but knew it was an answer to prayer as I would have more time. My generous and supportive husband, Tony, said I should manage the campaign as he "could not think of a better person."

I prayed as I did not know where to start. God would direct my steps as He had done before. I just needed to fully rely on Him for plans and direction. The first answer to my prayer was from a man named Gerald. He worked for the Greenville County School District and remarked, "What are you women doing? Do you not know that Duke McCall is a giant?"

My mind immediately went to a story I read about a giant killer. I had to apologize to the people involved because my thoughts were not on the conversation.

I argued quietly with God, "I am not going to throw stones at our opponent!" There must be another way to defeat a "giant."

I quickly reasoned with God that Julie's last name was "Hershey." The small stones could be Hershey's Kisses!" After all, we had no money to run a campaign. I would just ask friends and members of our Sunday school class to donate a bag of Hershey's Kisses. I reasoned that our friends buy food. They were all happy to donate a small bag of candy to our campaign. I called the Hershey Company to get their permission. They gave it as long as they were not endorsing a campaign with their name. I assured them that they were not endorsing Julie, that Hershey's kisses was just a play on words. They laughed and agreed.

The next step was for Julie to print a flyer with her views. She did so at a minimal cost. We then had to reach all the voters in her district. I prayed again and asked God for direction. I remembered a verse from Deuteronomy. Deuteronomy was the expansion of the law given to Moses at Mt. Sinai. I went to the law book that was guiding my life now. I had recently purchased the *Walk Thru the Bible, Open Bible Expanded Edition* at a seminar held at my church. I wanted God to guide my life and spent much time perusing His Word so I could get directions. I had learned that God does not guide one in an manner inconsistent with how He has interacted with His people in the past.

In Deuteronomy 32:30, God is pronouncing judgment on Israel and says:

> How could one man pursue a thousand, or two put ten thousand to flight, unless their Rock had sold them, unless the LORD had given them up? (NIV)

This verse spoke to me and gave me direction. It wasn't about God's judgment, but it spoke to me because I asked for direction. There were 10,000 people in District 21.

I got it! God was telling me to have two women greet 10,000 by walking to their doors and handing them a Hershey's Kiss for name recognition and to taste something sweet. We were not going to throw stones but candy.

Julie and our friends distributed Julie's humble flyer with her views. We did not ask for money to run the campaign but asked friends to donate Hershey's Kisses. People in District 21 were generally happy that we walked up to their door and gave them a flyer. From that point on, most campaigns were "ground" campaigns. Who knows if our campaign set the new standard?

Another event that caused concern for us was a printed handout that was distributed in Greer, SC. It was hand-delivered to homes or paper boxes. The flyer contained many negative comments about Julie. I was concerned. I went to God's Word for instructions. I then remembered a verse about "confusing their tongues" (Gen. 11:7).

I prayed and asked God for instructions on how to combat the negative campaign flyer. I then prayed a simple prayer: "God confuse their tongues." He answered my prayer.

When I got one of the negative campaign flyers, I noticed a handwritten comment written across the top before it was copied and distributed. It said, "Beware of sheep in wolves' clothing!"

I laughed out loud and remarked, "The saying is 'Beware of wolves in sheep's clothing!'"

God had confused their tongues! No one would be afraid of a harmless-looking sheep but would be very afraid of a wolf! Their handwritten comment at the top of the flyer was confused!

We won with a large margin and little campaign funds. I knew God had directed us. The national press could not understand our victory. We were called "stealth candidates." We were accused of trying to take over school boards by a "religious right" group. [6] I just laughed at the negative press.

We were representing people who shared our views. We did not hide anything but exposed what was happening where our children spend most of their wakeful hours for five days a week. For four years Julie was criticized, but she stayed strong in her views.

31

Trailer Park

Our victory gained support, too. Greenville County was a conservative county, but most residents were busy serving church-supported ministries, not politics. My experience on Capitol Hill and my conversion experience while in Washington, DC made me see politics as stewardship of our nation's history and rich traditions.

I loved the written law, the U.S. Constitution, and the written law of God. As a historian, I read that the first law to allow for public education passed in Massachusetts (home and hotbed of the American Revolution). The Old Deluder Satan Act was passed in 1647.

Below are two descriptions. One is from the New England Historical Society, and the other is from Encyclopedia.com.

> Massachusetts asked every family to contribute a peck of grain every year to Harvard. Hundreds of New England families gave 'college corn' to support Harvard.
>
> In 1638, Thomas Hooker set up a Latin school in Hartford, now Hartford Public High School. In 1701, 10 ministers founded Yale College, 'for Publick employment both in Church & Civil State.'
>
> The Act, in fact, established the foundation for public schooling in America, according to historian David Carleton. It set out the principles that the responsibility for basic education belongs to the community or public, he wrote. It also established the principle that the state can require communities to pay for schools and to run them. Finally, it organized schools separating elementary from secondary education.[7]

"...being one of the chief projects of that old deluder Satan to keep men from the knowledge of the Scriptures." The legislation proper required that townships of 50 families or more appoint a common schoolmaster to teach reading...[8]

I believed this, taught it to history students, and was recognized for my teaching of accurate history. I also received a state award for community service.

We were given the first-ever Order of the Silver Crescent. The Order of the Silver Crescent is an award created by then-governor David Beasley in 1997 for those who exhibited exemplary community service.

The honor was presented to my SCS students and me by Governor David Beasley at the State of the State Address. Mary Wood, Governor Beasley's wife, found out how I drove a bus of students to help two homeless women and their families. The homeless women wandered into a class I was teaching at SCS. We arranged for their lunch. My students then decided to help the women in multiple ways. We collected funds for the women to rent a mobile home. We also collected funds to refurbish and furnish the trailer. Our students arranged for the women to get jobs at McDonald's and watched their children while they worked. The "Trailer Park" ministry spread to the SCS high school and to the other trailers in the park. Our SCS students cleaned the trailer park and played games with the residents. I drove the bus to take students to Simpsonville every Thursday for months that fall semester in 1994.

We did not help the ladies for recognition or awards. We helped them out of genuine compassion. Our three sons had this ethic, too.

32

One Friday Night

Late one Friday night, I received a visit from South Carolina State Representative Mike Easterday (District 27) and his wife. This visit was perhaps prompted by Julie's unlikely campaign victory, or the two political recognitions mentioned in the previous chapter or my political activism in Greenville County or perhaps even the Lord's direct communication. Whatever prompted them, they appeared at my front door.

Mike and Mrs. Easterday told Tony and me that the Lord directed them to tell me that I should run for the South Carolina State House. I objected because I was better at serving others so they could be great. I did not want to run in my own election. Tony then stopped me and said we needed to ask God and family what they wanted. I stopped objecting and agreed to pray and seek counsel.

Our family was consulted after we prayed. One hundred percent of family members said I should run. We took it as a sign from God. I agreed to run for the South Carolina State House District 27 even though I was just a little Christian school history teacher. At this point, I knew that if God was for me, who could be against me (Rom. 8:31)?

The special election was going to be held in April. It was in January when the Easterday's visited my home and told us that the governor had tapped Mike to work in the governor's legislative department. He had to resign from his position as a legislator in the South Carolina State House as a result of the governor tapping Mike.

We had to raise money, select a campaign staff and volunteers, make ads, attend debates, and put out signs to run in a special election. I knew what was involved in a political campaign and knew it was going to be busy, but I knew God would guide and direct my path if He wanted me to run and win in this campaign.

As usual, Tony was my finance manager. He said we raised about $10,000 in a short time. Tony then used his Excel skills and organized our campaign. Mary Swain—my official manager, my friend, and a parent of one of my history students—organized much. My friend, Becky Reid, hosted the results party at her home that was organized by Mary.

We basically had a great time running the campaign. Becky Reid hosted, and Mary Swain ran the campaign. There were many students who volunteered to help as I was still teaching AP European History at the time. They volunteered on their own time after school and without me asking them. They wanted to help and thought it was cool that their teacher was running for the South Carolina Legislature. Many attended the candidate debate in Simpsonville.

There were four candidates who ran. The governor asked Mike Easterday to not endorse a candidate. The debate was fun to me, and my friend, Senator David Thomas, helped prepare me for it. I frequently thought of the debates I would watch as my daddy discussed politics and current events. It was hard to believe that this Hispanic school teacher participated in a political debate. It was exhilarating to me.

Anyway, I won the special election. There were four candidates in the race, and the winner needed to obtain 50% + 1 of the votes. I only received 34.1% so the two top vote-getters had to compete in a run-off. Garry Smith received the next highest number of votes and gained 28.5% of the votes. Garry and I were headed to a run-off election. I had never done that before.

My AP history students and their parents had received my promise that I would guide them to pass the difficult AP exam in early May. It was important to me that I kept my word to them. We would use the Easter break to prepare for the exam. After all, my campaign manager would be out of town, and we would not campaign.[9]

So, I decided not to campaign during the two weeks prior to the run-off campaign. One hundred percent of my students passed, but we lost in the run-off campaign by 101 votes. I knew the election loss was a possibility because I had not campaigned. I called and congratulated Garry, who won. Garry served for 20 years in the South Carolina Legislature and remains a good friend though he recently retired to help family in Aiken, South Carolina. I often wondered if I did not obey God's calling. Tony frequently replied, "God is just preparing you for something bigger."

One Friday Night

He was right.

33

James Madison Memorial Fellowship

As usual, Tony said there was a reason I did not win in the run-off election. I was initially disappointed because I believed I could win but had not campaigned because it was close in time to AP exams. I had committed to my students and their parents that I would guide them to success on the exam. God had a reason that I ran, won, and then lost.

Tony advised that I just trust God. I reflected on the campaign and tried to take it back from God. Should I have campaigned to win the run-off? It would have meant I violated my commitment to students and their parents. I knew I could not do that even if there were only a few students.

Well, Tony was right, again, about trusting God's plan. I had applied but never expected to receive the James Madison Memorial Fellowship. I applied anyway.

The James Madison Memorial Fellowship Foundation's website lists the criteria. I had applied following eligibility qualifications for applicants:

> Fellowship applicants compete only against other applicants from the state of their legal residence. To be eligible to apply for a fellowship, you must:
>
> - Be a U.S. citizen.
>
> - Be a teacher, or plan to become a teacher, of American history, American government, or civics classes where you will teach topics on the Constitution at the secondary school level (grades 7–12)

- Possess a bachelor's degree or plan to receive a bachelor's degree no later than August 31 of the year in which you are applying[10]

James Madison Fellowships were created to honor Madison's legacy and Madisonian principles by providing support for graduate study that focuses on the Constitution—its history and contemporary relevance to the practices and policies of democratic government. The benefits of the fellowship program are manifold and lasting. Fellowship recipients have a unique opportunity to strengthen their research, writing, and analytical skills. In the process, they form professional ties that can significantly influence their career aspirations. Fellows gain a deeper understanding of the principles of constitutional government, which they in turn transmit to their students. In this way, the James Madison Fellowships ensure that the spirit and practical wisdom of the Constitution will guide the actions of future generations of American citizens.[11]

The Fellowship was for $24,000. It was awarded with the stipulation that I get a master's degree and return to teach in the social studies department in a high school.

Those qualifications were easy to meet. I was told that being politically active helped the candidates. I applied as I met all the qualifications and was politically active. Then I received a phone call that changed my thinking. Tony had been right. God had another plan for me. Admiral Paul Yost called me on the phone.

Admiral Yost began our conversation with, "Congratulations, Mrs. Koury. You are officially the oldest recipient of the James Madison Memorial Fellowship."

I was 52 years old at the time. I had three grown college-graduated and employed sons. Our oldest was married and had children. How could this grandma qualify? I did, however, and the late Admiral Yost was proud to tell me the news. He congratulated me, and we hung up. I was pleased but in shock. I did not expect the Fellowship, but the desire of my heart was to study the U.S. Constitution.

I kept thinking of the verse I memorized while in California.

But seek first the kingdom of God and his righteousness, and all these things will be added to you. (Matt. 6:33 ESV)

My task following the call from Admiral Yost was to find a college that had strong academic courses in government and the U.S. Constitution. It was also recommended that we find a college that did not require a master's degree thesis paper. Many JMM Fellows did not complete their degree because of the thesis paper.

Converse College in Spartanburg, South Carolina, met these requirements. I was immediately impressed with their course offerings and their professors. Converse's website describes the program description as follows:

- Veteran Faculty: Our faculty have extensive experience in public education as teachers, administrators, or special consultants.

- Quality Education: Our curriculum is aligned with professional standards and meets all the requirements for national approvals by the Council for Accreditation for Educator Preparation (CAEP), approved by the South Carolina Department of Education. You will be qualified for certification reciprocity with many other states.

- Community Partnerships: We enjoy close proximity to and partnerships with local public schools enabling you to have diverse experiences in a variety of schools while introducing you to a broad spectrum of student populations and work opportunities. These partnerships place social studies teacher candidates with master teachers for clinical and student teaching placements.[12]

What impressed me about Converse College the most was the head of the History and Politics Department and all the professors. I was also impressed with the leadership roles held by students, including their discipline code and their student pledge that they did not cheat.

Converse College's mission also impressed me. It is to help students "see clearly, decide wisely, and act justly."

We raised our three sons and guided them through their college experience. I knew I would not get another degree until they graduated. God provided the money and the perfect timing. I loved college.

I loved learning and fulfilled all my requirements including completing the Summer Institute on the U.S. Constitution at Georgetown

University in Washington, DC. I loved being back in DC again and walking the streets of Georgetown. I loved the history of the city and the history of our country. I loved studying the U.S. Constitution, the U.S. presidents, and the three branches of government. I loved learning from Dr. Herman Belz and Dr. Jeffrey Morrison.

It was such a great experience for this Hispanic woman who was not even supposed to go to college. My high school guidance counselor would be shocked at my academic success. Not only had I graduated from college with a bachelor's degree but was enrolled in a master's degree program. He would be surprised that not only had this Hispanic female gone to college, worked as a teacher and for a U.S. Senator but even maintained good grades in both undergraduate and graduate studies.

Tony decided it was time to sell our big house in Riverwalk and move to Converse Heights in Spartanburg across from Converse College. We sold our home after seventeen years. We moved to Spartanburg, a small community thirty miles north of Greenville. I lived at home and walked to college daily. Converse College was across the street from our home in Converse Heights. It took only ten minutes to walk to class. I loved it.

Our nine years in Spartanburg were memorable. We saw two sons get married and one of them had a child. Tony was very supportive of my college career and used his gifts to help others. He gave unselfishly to whoever needed help. God proved that you cannot outgive Him.

My generous husband gave money to many needy people in exchange for yard work while we lived in Spartanburg. He also sold his 1986 Mercedes with 250,000 miles on it to a deaf man. I will never forget that day as the Mercedes was driven by our sons and had been in the family for about 20 years. It is a neat story.

One day a girl came to our door in Spartanburg off of Main Street. She called her boyfriend, Malcolm, who wanted to inquire about the Mercedes. She was mute and deaf, so she wrote her inquiry. Tony told her the Mercedes was not for sale. A few months later, Tony advertised it on social media as for sale by owner. Our sons were in shock and disappointed. The Mercedes was part of our family. They borrowed it to date and go to college.

An interpreter for Malcolm saw the ad. He said Malcolm was still interested in the Mercedes. Malcolm came to our home in Spartanburg and loved the Mercedes. Tony sold it to Malcolm for $4,000, and Malcolm drove off. Tony and Malcolm became friends and wrote by e-mail often. The last e-mail Tony received from Malcolm was from New York City. Malcom wrote, "Mercedes and I are enjoying the sites in New York City."

34

SCS Again

We loved our home in Spartanburg. We loved our church and our neighborhood. We had every intention of staying in Spartanburg.

The millionaire and textile giant, Roger Milliken, would walk by our house often. He wore a name tag (as if people did not know who he was). Milliken would always attend our Converse Heights Republican Precinct meetings. He would arrive early and always have a proposal that we would vote upon. Wikipedia describes Milliken as:

> an American **textile heir**, industrialist, **businessman, and political activist.** He served as President and then CEO of his family's company, Milliken & Company, from 1947 until 2005. He continued to serve as Chairman of the Board until his death in 2010. (emphasis added)[13]

I attended the Spartanburg County Convention of the Republican Party and wrote a resolution to honor our neighbor. Milliken was properly honored for his contribution to economics and politics in Spartanburg County and the United States.

We were happy living in Spartanburg. I was going to teach at a local public school with my new master's degree after graduating from Converse College.

The principal told me that all social studies teachers must also coach a sport. I was not keen on coaching a sport. I think I could have coached volleyball or softball because I played both. I played volleyball in high school and stopped playing softball about ten years earlier.

Actually, Tony insisted I stop playing softball when I slid into second base, and he yelled, "You are the mother of our sons! What are you doing?"

Maybe it was the game before when I was a substitute pitcher for the Michelin Tire Women's Softball Team. When I showed up to pitch, I was informed by our coach that the catcher was not there. I was asked to substitute for that position. *Well*, I thought, *I put on catcher's gear and caught the pitched ball when one of our sons was a high school pitcher.*

"Sure," I replied to a desperate coach. I put on the catcher's facemask and pads.

The game went well until a German BMW woman approached the plate. I said a prayer that this Amazon-looking six-foot-plus female would strike out. She did not strike out. I then prayed that she would be thrown out at first base. She was not thrown out at first or second bases. I had a decision to make when I was faced with the inevitable. I had committed to play catcher. One of my jobs was to protect home plate. I prayed again that she would be thrown out as she rounded third base. She was not thrown out at third. *Oh well*, I thought. *I will die here. I will defend the home plate at all costs.*

The BMW player rounded third base and charged at home plate to score a run. I was going to cover my base no matter what. She pushed me off of home plate and shoved me toward the backstop. I slid down the backstop and realized I still had the softball in my mitt. She was called "out" by the umpire. I felt relieved. Tony was watching, and Tony was very upset. I also felt proud that I held my ground. I was happy that Tony was watching and cheering. I felt relieved that I got the BMW player out at home. But I knew that my days playing softball after age 45 were limited.

No, I would not agree to coach a team as a social studies teacher. I then applied and was offered a teaching position at Spartanburg Day School. Spartanburg Day was an elite private school. We had played them in sports when our sons played in high school. I knew the school and liked the offer. I would teach at another private school.

As I was preparing to teach at Spartanburg Day School, Don Kauffman, the new Southside Christian School (SCS) high school principal, called me. He made an offer that I could not refuse because of the salary, benefits, and schedule. I returned to teach high school history at SCS though I would remain in Spartanburg and commute. I knew God was directing my path. I just had to join Him.

35

23rd Psalm

One of our sons lived out of town. The Lord prompted me one Friday night to visit him. I am glad I obeyed the prompting of the Spirit. The next morning, I rushed him to the emergency room. The 23rd psalm ministered to me during this trying time.

Our pastor from First Baptist North Spartanburg visited that night. So did his brothers and some of my fellow teachers. It took weeks before the doctor released him.

During the time our son was in the hospital, I memorized the 23rd psalm. The King James Version says,

> The LORD is my shepherd; I shall not want.
> He maketh me to lie down in green pastures: he leadeth me
> beside the still waters.
> He restoreth my soul: he leadeth me in the paths of right-
> eousness for his name's sake.
> Yea, though I walk through the valley of the shadow of
> death, I will fear no evil: for thou art with me; thy rod and
> thy staff they comfort me.
> Thou preparest a table before me in the presence of mine en-
> emies: thou anointest my head with oil; my cup runneth
> over.
> Surely goodness and mercy shall follow me all the days of
> my life: and I will dwell in the house of the LORD forever.

Every time our son was wheeled back for surgery, I said this psalm over him and pleaded with God to save our son. I visualized that the "rod" of the doctor and the "staff" of the Good Shepherd would sustain his life.

It did. Our God was faithful to answer prayer and assured me that things would be okay. Once again, God heard prayers and responded.

Matt's wife took good care of him so I returned to teaching Advanced Placement (AP) European, then AP World, and, ultimately, AP United States History. We still lived in Spartanburg, and I drove down Interstate Highway 85 for 30 minutes daily. I was offered a substitute professorship of U.S. History at both Converse College and the University of South Carolina at the Upstate campus. I took both jobs. I enjoyed teaching both courses and was grateful to Dr. Kauffman at Southside Christian School (SCS) that I was able to teach at three places. I loved teaching history.

I used to take my high school SCS AP History students to a local coffee shop near SCS when we studied the Pacific Islands of Sumatra and Java in the Industrial Revolution. We would have Sumatra or Java and discuss the Pacific Island's role in the Industrial Revolutions.

On our way back to the school on Woodruff Road I noticed a neighborhood I had never seen before. I was driving the small school bus and excitedly asked the students, "When did that neighborhood appear?"

One student chuckled and replied, "Mrs. Koury, it has been there about ten years!"

I usually did not travel east of Woodruff Road, but that year, I took my history students to Java Bistro, a relatively new coffee shop on East Woodruff Road. That neighborhood might not have actually been new, but it was new to me. I *knew* I just had to visit it.

My next class was going to start soon so I thought that there was no way I could take the students back, get my car, and visit the neighborhood. Still, I just *knew* I had to visit the neighborhood right away. So, I ignored the logical voices in my head. I listened to the other voices and took the students back, exchanged the small bus for my car, and drove to the "new-to-me" neighborhood called Asheton Lakes.

Once I entered the neighborhood, I was drawn to a small home that was for sale. I called the realtor after I read the phone number on the sign in the yard. The realtor described the house, and I knew it would not work. Besides I thought, *I have to teach a class soon!* Still, I could not leave the neighborhood without looking more. I *knew* I was supposed to be there.

I called another realtor from a sign on the front yard as I drove around. The realtor told me that she was showing a house at the end of a cul-de-sac to a prospective buyer but would show me another house for sale when she was finished.

At this point, I was still driving around the neighborhood and asked her to describe her car. She did, and we discovered that I was on the same street. As I drove around the cul-de-sac, the 23rd psalm that I had memorized years before hit me like a ton of bricks. I passed a "green pasture," "still waters" and "the path of righteousness."

The path or sidewalk behind our house that ran along the lake led to Southside Christian School where I could freely teach about the righteousness of the Lord.

I argued out loud as I drove around. "I have to teach a class in a few minutes. I cannot keep looking!" Then I saw a small sign near the pasture, water, and path. It was a "Lot for Sale" sign.

Again, I argued out loud to the Spirit that was directing me. "But I have to teach a class in a few minutes!" I suppressed my feelings and was obedient to my promptings. I called the number by the bushes on the lot.

Mr. Brian Lazarus answered the call right away. I asked him if the plot of land in Asheton Lakes was still for sale.

Lazarus replied. "Yes, it is, to the right buyer."

I said, "You just found the right buyer. I have just one problem," I told him. "My husband has no idea I am here.. Can Tony come to see the lot?"

"Sure. When should I expect him?" asked Mr. Lazarus.

Tony was surprised by my call but had learned that God speaks to me regularly. Our sons and their families had recently moved back to Greenville. Tony and I had discussed moving back to Greenville, too, but dismissed the idea because we loved Spartanburg. We both had jobs in Greenville but reasoned that our commute would be just as long as we fought the traffic in Greenville. We did not discuss a move again until that day.

I told Mr. Lazarus that I would call Tony right away and let them arrange a time to see the lot. I called Tony on my way back to school to teach.

Tony agreed to see the lot. He was confused, however. When he had suggested that we build a house in Greenville, I had excitedly exclaimed, "I am not going to build another house!"

Now I was asking him to see a lot and build a house. This led to his confusion, but he agreed to drive down Highway 14 to see the lot right away. He left Michelin International Headquarters where he worked and drove to see the lot.

"It is spectacular," Tony exclaimed when he saw the lot. "The view is beautiful!" He called Brian right away and wanted to go by his office and give him earnest money to hold the lot. Mr. Lazarus told Tony that he would not take his downpayment until Tony walked the lot because it was an unusual shape. Brian told Tony that it was hard to build on the lot because it was a triangle shape. Tony said he could design a house on the lot. He was very creative. He had artistic skills like his dad. We bought the lot.

Immediately, I thought about Brian's comment and thought to myself. *Hmm ... a triangle has three sides. The Godhead has three parts. The Father, Son, and Holy Spirit.* I knew God, again, was directing my path. Although Lazarus was a Jewish name and my Savior was a Jew, I kept my thoughts to myself as I did not think they would understand my thought processes.

Within weeks, our new purchase became a family project. First with Andy, one of our twins, , then Lindsay, our daughter-in-law, who designed a floor plan. She designed it one night on a paper towel. She is very creative and designed a model exactly like I wanted it.

Tony then took the floor plan designed by Lindsay and put the plan in an Excel document. He color-coded each room. When he presented our design to Brian, our builder, Brian remarked, "You want me to build you a LEGO house?"

Tony is very creative. Tony designed and built all three of our sons' cribs. He is a great craftsman. Our first son's crib did not have any nails. Tony used cut dowel rods for nails. He got the idea for a spiral staircase we had visited at a church in Santa Fe, New Mexico. Legend has it that the helix-shaped spiral staircase was built miraculously by a mysterious carpenter named Joseph after they prayed for nine days to St. Joseph. Tony took ideas and created. I knew from past experiences that Tony could design my house on a triangular lot. He did.

We built the house in a triangular shape. To be honest, it is our dream home. We are not moving again until God calls us Home.

Epilogue

There are more accolades given to me including the Greenville News' "Teacher of the Week," Wal-Mart Corporation's "Teacher of the Year," Who's Who Among America's Teachers, Multi-Year AP Reader, and others. Suffice it to say, I have been blessed. This Hispanic woman who was told that "my type did not go to college" earned several educational honors. God has directed my path. I am a New Mexican who found a personal Savior and never returned to New Mexico.

When I think of my blessings in life, I cannot help but cry at the direction and purpose God has given to my life after I surrendered it to Him. I am overwhelmed. I am at peace with whatever life has for me. I am thankful for the blessings God has given to me. Daddy would be proud of his "I baby."

God has crowned me with victory in this life and the next. My daddy would honor his queen if he and my mom were still living. I will see them again though. That is my belief and my joy. They both experienced pain in life and made poor decisions, but they are at peace now. So am I. I know for certain where they are.

In Hebrews 11:1, it describes faith. "Now faith is confidence in what we hope for and assurance about what we do not see" (NIV). I have that confidence I will see my parents again.

As the late Sue Kennedy taught me, there is a roaring lion, the devil, seeking someone to devour. It is true. We live in a spiritual world, and we are only passing through. My life has been devoted to the Good Spirit since He possessed me so many years ago.

Today, as a retired educator, I serve as a community leader on a board, a council, and a club chaplain. I am a substitute teacher and an adult Bible teacher. I enjoy spending time with nearby grandkids and enjoy the house on the lake that God gave to us. I am ready to meet Him with my dad and mom in Heaven when God calls me home.

Citations

[1] Juliet White, "There's A Tiny Town In New Mexico Completely Surrounded By Breathtaking Natural Beauty," *Only in Your State,* February 28, 2017, www.onlyinyourstate.com/new-mexico/tiny-town-natural-beauty-nm/.

[2] "Santa Rosa de Lima and Santo Tomás de Apostle: A Chronological Essay," Saint Thomas the Apostle Catholic Parish, October 2, 2023, www.stthomasabiquiu.com/santa-rose-de-lima-chapel.

[3] Barbara Maranzani, "Martin Luther King Jr. and Malcolm X Only Met Once," Biography, January 19, 2021, www.biography.com/activists/martin-luther-king-jr-malcolm-x-meeting.

[4] Lea Carpenter, "In Tragedy, Kennedy Quoted Aeschylus," Big Think, January 11, 2011, bigthink.com/the-present/in-tragedy-kennedy-quoted-aeschylus/.

[5] "Covenant Life Church," Wikipedia, October 6, 2023, https://en.wikipedia.org/wiki/Covenant_Life_Church.

[6] "Parent Who Shuns School Wins Board Seat," *The New York Times,* December 7, 1992, www.nytimes.com/1992/12/27/us/parent-who-shuns-school-wins-board-seat.html?smid=em-share.

[7] "How The Old Deluder Satan Act Made Sure Puritan Children Got Educated," *New England Historical Society,* October 9, 2023, https://newenglandhistoricalsociety.com/old-deluder-satan-act-made-sure-puritan-children-got-educated.

[8] "Old Deluder Satan Act," *Encyclopedia.com,* October 9, 2023, https://www.encyclopedia.com/religion/encyclopedias-almanacs-transcripts-and-maps/old-deluder-satan-act.

[9] https://www.ourcampaigns.com/RaceDetail.html?RaceID=239094, https://www.ourcampaigns.com/RaceDetail.html?RaceID=239095

[10] Eligibility Requirements, James Madison Memorial Fellowship Foundation, October 2, 2023, www.jamesmadison.gov/fellowship-information/fellowship-eligibility.

[11] "About the Foundation," James Madison Memorial Fellowship Foundation, October 2, 2023, https://www.jamesmadison.gov/foundation-information/about.

[12] About Converse, Converse, October 2, 2023, www.converse.edu/about/.

[13] "Roger Milliken," *Wikipedia, October 9, 2023, https://en.wikipedia.org/wiki/Roger_Milliken.*

Made in the USA
Columbia, SC
17 January 2024

29659591R00098